# TENNESSEE LITERARY LUMINARIES

# TENNESSEE LITERARY LUMINARIES

## FROM CORMAC McCARTHY TO ROBERT PENN WARREN

SUE FREEMAN CULVERHOUSE

THE History PRESS

Published by The History Press
Charleston, SC 29403
www.historypress.net



First published 2013

Manufactured in the United States

ISBN 978.1.60949.830.6

Library of Congress CIP data applied for.

*To Bill*

# CONTENTS

# PREFACE

I wrote this book out of love of reading and the insane idea that I could study and learn enough about at least ten Tennessee writers in a year to create a worthwhile book. After reading scores of books, articles and websites, plus talking to numerous people, I'm certain what results occurred were possible only through the help of a great many other people.

I've been a freelance writer since 1976. I decided in January of that year that if I could sell an article within that calendar year, I'd begin writing as often as I could. I sold my first article, "The Truth about Orchids," to *Flower and Garden* magazine in February and never looked back. I've written for numerous magazines, several newspapers (even won a couple of Virginia Press Awards during the year when I wrote for the daily, Waynesboro *News-Virginian)* and have published a self-help book, *Seven Keys to a Successful Life*. I've taught writing not only in public schools but also to teachers and in colleges. My students created a literary magazine that featured all-student writing and illustrations—someone even listed one of the copies on Amazon.

In addition, I have met a number of these people about whom I have written. Of course, I never met Robert Penn "Red" Warren, Cormac McCarthy (who doesn't like to talk to other writers), Alex Haley or Eleanor Ross Taylor. Warren and Haley were dead before I ever dreamed of this book. I included Cormac McCarthy not only for his brilliant writing but also because he was kind to William Gay and helped William on his path to publication. I did meet Peter Taylor when I lived in Charlottesville, Virginia, when he used to go to Sunday afternoons at the home of Eddy von Selzam on Wayside Place; Peter and Eleanor lived across the street from Eddy at one time. However, I never met Eleanor during those years because that sort of gathering was not something she attended.

I was able to meet William Gay, Alice Randall, A. Scott Pearson, Amy Greene and Marshall Chapman—all beautiful people in addition to having contributed literature not to be missed. I met Bud Willis after having read and reviewed *Marble Mountain*; Bud had a book signing in Clarksville, after which his lovely wife, Lee, and he became my friends.

I chose all of these people because their books are meaningful to me. When I was a sixth grader at Moore Elementary School in Clarksville and spent as much time in the school library as possible, I decided that the only road to immortality was becoming an author. Books live long after those who write them and mark history as nothing else does.

One of the joys of writing this book has been learning of the historical events that influenced several of these writers. For instance, the Night Riders are featured in the work of at least four of these people. The influence of one writer on another was also a revelation to me. The longer one lives, the more often one sees that events are like ripples in the water that eventually touch others in unexpected ways.

Every year, I attend the Clarksville Writers' Conference at Austin Peay University (APSU) in Clarksville, Tennessee. In 2012, I listened to remarks by Keven McQueen, during which he told his listeners that if they ever considered writing a nonfiction book, they should get in contact with The History Press in Charleston, South Carolina. He said that they are wonderful people with whom to work.

A few weeks after this conference, I did just that. Fortunately for me, I reached Banks Smither and the rest is history. Banks has been terrific in helping me through this project, as has his assistant, Alyssa Pierce. Their suggestions improved this manuscript immeasurably. It has been my great fortune to have Julia Turner as editor for this manuscript; she has translated what I attempted to say into what I meant to say, and I am eternally grateful for her efforts in my behalf.

I am also deeply indebted to Bill Larson and Mark Haynes of *Clarksville Online*. Bill's photographs are an integral part of this book. The technical assistance of both Bill and Mark has been critical to the manuscript and photographs being transmitted in a readable fashion. They created my website to showcase *Tennessee Literary Luminaries* and have been supportive with all my endeavors. I have been writing for *Clarksville Online* for several years and have found both these young men to be exceptional in their dedication to journalism and the visual arts..

Every writer knows that librarians are writer's friends. Scott Shumate in the Special Collections of the Felix G. Woodward Library at APSU has gone above and beyond in helping locate information on Robert Penn Warren. Mary Ann Meyers and everyone in the Reference Department of the Montgomery County Public Library in Clarksville were also extremely helpful. Amy Lewellen of the Customs House Museum was gracious in attempting to locate information for me at the museum. Teresa Gray, public services archivist for Special Collections and University Archives at Vanderbilt University, went to extensive research to locate letters from Peter Taylor and Eleanor Ross Taylor in the Jean and Alexander Heard Library. Kyle Hovious of Special Collections in the Hodges Library at the University of Tennessee worked diligently with me so that I could have pictures of Cormac McCarthy and Alex Haley. Jocelyn Triplett of the Digitization Services Department at the University of Virginia Library assisted in making available pictures of Peter Taylor. Sandra Stacey of the Montgomery County Archives (Department of Preservation and Records) was also instrumental in locating information on Warren and those involved with him at Clarksville High School.

Special appreciation goes to Paula Boger, director, and Beverly Johnson, program coordinator, of the Alex Haley Museum and Interpretive Center in Henning, Tennessee as well as to Magnolia Murray Johnson for sharing information on the life of Alex Haley.

J.M. (Michael) White, a close friend of William Gay and publisher at Wild Dog Press, generously allowed me to use his pictures not only of William and his artwork but also of the homes of Cormac McCarthy in Knoxville. Shelia Kennedy, who is typing up the difficult-to-read unpublished manuscripts of William Gay, has been a true friend and most helpful during this entire project. William's sons, Chris and William, have also been kind in assisting me with information and memories of their father. Others who have shared memories include Sonny Brewer, Tom Franklin and Marshall Chapman—thanks to all!

Professor Wes Berry of Western Kentucky University has been forthcoming with information from the RPW Circle and has included me in the Circle sessions at APSU and in Guthrie. I was able to meet Warren scholars such as William Bedford Clark, editor of the Warren documents, and to speak with others who actually knew Warren and have made lifelong studies of his work.

Others who have been most generous with their time and expertise include Patricia Winn, founder of the Clarksville Writers' Conference, and her husband, Howard Winn, professor emeritus of history at APSU; Christopher Burawa, director of the Center of Excellence for the Creative Arts at Austin Peay State University; Professor William Bedford Clark of the Department of English at Texas A&M University and general editor of the Robert Penn Warren Correspondence Project; and Keven McQueen, instructor in the Department of English and Theater at Eastern Kentucky University and author of many books. All these people have been most encouraging and have given their time to help me in my research.

Two of my cousins, Jerry Abernathy Church and Betty Williams Chesney, have provided moral support, housing for research trips and willing ears during this project. My aunts, Ione Crosslin Williams, Margaret Crosslin Estes and Mozelle Crosslin Abernathy, have also provided generous love and support in all my endeavors.

My mother, Vera Crosslin Freeman, has, as always, been supportive in numerous ways from beginning to end. At eighty-eight, she is an ever-willing ear for issues that arise and a helping hand when I need one. My brother and sister-in-law, Charles and Carol Freeman, are contributors to my life on a daily basis, and I am truly blessed to have such a great family.

My daughter, Susan Leigh Miller, a teacher in the Creative Writing Program of the Department of Arts and Sciences at Rutgers University, has a distinguished writing career of her own, including poems in the *Iowa Review*, *Black Warrior Review*, *Calyx*, *Meridian*, *Commonweal*, *Sewanee Theological Review*, *Portable Book Reader 4* and *Pollifax*. She was a semifinalist for the 2009 Kinereth Gensler Award, a finalist for the 2009 Autumn House Poetry Prize and the winner of the 2009 Dorothy Sargent Rosenberg Prize. A new mother, Susan has assisted me with numerous research items, and I am most grateful for her help.

My beloved husband, Bill, who has a juris doctorate with a twenty-seven-year law practice behind him and a distinguished career as a sculptor, has been my reader, my editor and the impetus to keep on keeping on when obstacles rose. He believes in me when I have little faith in myself and is the love of my life.

It is my hope that readers of *Tennessee Literary Luminaries* will not only learn about these outstanding Tennessee writers but will then read their unforgettable books.

SUE FREEMAN CULVERHOUSE
*Springfield, Tennessee*
*Summer 2013*

CHAPTER ONE

# ROBERT PENN WARREN AND HIS CLARKSVILLE CONNECTIONS

*You don't choose a story; it chooses you.*
*Robert Penn Warren*

Numerous books and articles have been written about writer Robert Penn Warren, but few have emphasized his time at Clarksville High School in Clarksville, Tennessee. Yet the time before and after that turning point in his life led to his remarkable writing career.

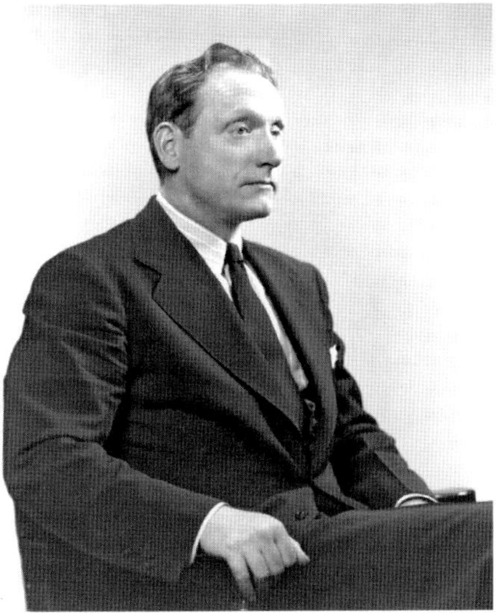

Robert Penn Warren. *Courtesy of Special Collections Library, Western Kentucky University.*

Born on April 24, 1905, in Guthrie, Kentucky, Robert Penn Warren was the oldest of three children of Robert Franklin Warren, a businessman and banker, and Anna Ruth Penn Warren, a schoolteacher. His siblings were Mary and Thomas. At home, this child, who would some day be a world-famous writer, was called "Rob'Penn" by his family or "Rob" by his friends.

## The Black Patch War

In *A Portrait of a Father*, the biography of his father, Robert Penn Warren described his own childhood and the life within his family.

Guthrie was the scene, in September 1904, of twenty-five thousand visitors "on horseback, in carriages, in farm wagons, on foot—there for the founding of the Black Fired Tobacco Association to combat price-fixing agreements among tobacco manufacturers." This later led to the "Tobacco War" or "the Black Patch War." Robert Penn said that he had a photograph of that event. This episode in history became the subject of Robert Penn Warren's first novel, *Night Rider*.

The reason Guthrie was chosen for this momentous meeting was that five railroad lines met in there: the Louisville & Nashville Railroad's (L&N) St. Louis–Evansville–Nashville line, the L&N Louisville-Memphis line, the L&N Guthrie–Bowling Green branch, the Edgefield and Kentucky Railroad and the Guthrie-Elkton (Kentucky) spur.

Tobacco growers formed the Dark Tobacco District Planters' Protective Association of Kentucky and Tennessee (PPA) on September 24, 1904 (the fall before Robert Penn was born in April 1905). The purpose of the group was to market tobacco. There are two types of tobacco: dark fired and burley. Until about 1924, burley was grown in eastern Tennessee, but eventually, sixty-six of the ninety-five counties in Tennessee depended on tobacco for one of their main cash crops. Of the eight counties in Tennessee that grew dark fired tobacco, Montgomery County (the location of Clarksville) was the second-largest producer in the state. Throughout most of their histories, Montgomery County and Clarksville have been well known for production of dark fired tobacco, a primary cash crop for locals.

Tobacco has been such an important part of Clarksville's financial history that it is featured in the rose window of Trinity Episcopal Church, a house of worship in downtown Clarksville since June 1832. Panes of glass that look like the hands of tobacco are featured in the window alongside corn sprouts; in the center of the window is what appears to be a dollar sign, reminding churchgoers of the importance tobacco money played in creating the church and its architecture.

Dark fired tobacco is primarily used for smokeless products, such as chewing tobacco, pipe tobacco and snuff, while burley goes into cigarettes. (Of course, the dangers of using tobacco were unknown in the 1920s.)

The areas of western Kentucky and northern Tennessee where dark fired tobacco was grown became known as the "black patch." The ensuing Black

Patch War brought on by a prolonged depression from falling tobacco prices became a serious threat to civil government as the PPA pressured all tobacco growers to join so that everyone would refuse to sell any tobacco until the purchasing companies agreed to raise prices. Those who would not join were called "hillbillies," and the buyers' monopoly (the American Tobacco Company and the Italian Regie) was called "the Trust." Some growers became vigilantes and were called the "Night Riders."

A group in Robertson County (the county with the largest output of dark fired tobacco) met and formed the Possum Hunters Organization, the purpose of which was to visit Trust tobacco buyers and hillbillies in groups of no less than five and no more than two thousand and convince them to adhere to the PPA using "peaceful" means. This spread to other counties, and a secret fraternity called the "Silent Brigade," or "Inner Circle," began attacking people and property, destroying tobacco in the fields, burning barns and warehouses, dynamiting farm machinery and killing livestock. Montgomery and Robertson Counties, western Kentucky and the towns of Hopkinsville, Russellville and Princeton were scenes of spectacular violence especially between 1907 and 1909.

The headquarters for the Dark Tobacco District Planters' Protective Association of Kentucky and Tennessee was located in Guthrie. At one point, the governor of Kentucky sent troops into Guthrie to attempt to quell some of the violence brought about by the Night Riders. Robert Franklin Warren had taken Robert Penn when he was but an infant to see "troops putting up their tents in an open section near the railroad station."

In *Night Rider*, Robert Penn Warren relates how he grew up in a world of violence that he accepted as part of life. He heard about it, saw fights and felt there was no way out.

When World War I began in 1914, the Night Riders ceased their activity, not only because Kentucky troops were dispatched against them but also because civil suits against some were won and tobacco prices rose.

It is no surprise that Robert Penn Warren set his novel *Night Rider*, based on this terrifying time, in the areas of Guthrie and Clarksville, the two towns with which he was most familiar during his childhood.

Robert Penn Warren actually uses a quotation from his father as the words of his *Night Rider* character Dr. MacDonald when he states his beliefs about white people who blame African Americans for their "bad luck." Robert Penn Warren might have used unacceptable terms when his characters spoke, but at home, no one was allowed to use the *n* word. His father forbade it and assured all within his hearing that he had rarely met anyone of any color who would not try to treat you right if you treated him right.

Of course, the language used in some of Warren's writing is the racist language of the day, and every reader must be aware that none of his characters is concerned in the least about being "politically correct" according to today's standards. That just wasn't the way things were in Warren's time. Later claims that Warren was a racist were based on that language but did not take into consideration that he wrote two books, *Segregation: The Inner Conflict in the South* (a discussion of attitudes long-held by Southerners concerning race) and *Who Speaks for the Negro?* (interviews with leaders of the civil rights movement), that could not be considered racist volumes.

## EARLY CHILDHOOD

*I remember an overwhelming passionate desire to write a poem when I was twelve years old and had a fever.*
*Robert Penn Warren*

Robert Penn entered Guthrie School when he was six and continued there (where there were some very good teachers, he insisted) until he was fifteen. His summers were usually spent at the farm of his maternal grandfather in Kentucky.

Having met in Clarksville and married in 1904, Robert Penn's parents seemed, to him, to always be in private conversation together. His memories of them were often of their walking or sitting with their heads slightly bent toward each other. He claimed he never learned what it was that they were talking about.

The reason Robert Franklin moved from Clarksville to Guthrie was the promise of a newfound prosperity there, as the crossing of north–south and east–west railroads brought twenty-two trains a day. Also, two new banks and three saloons were part of the attractions.

Robert Penn said he never heard a cross word between his parents and that his mother had claimed that a happy marriage was simple because everything outside the front gate belonged to her husband and everything inside belonged to her.

Robert Franklin Warren believed that education was the only salvation for democracy, according to Robert Penn, and therefore, he served on the school board in Guthrie.

Both parents provided for the interests of all three of their children as they progressed from one hobby to another.

Robert Penn remembered having books appear alongside his current activities; for example, when a friend who was a woodsman engaged Robert Penn in tramping along on his hikes, the book *Two Little Savages and How They Grew* by Ernest Thompson Seton was suddenly part of Robert Penn's reading matter. When he became interested in bird watching, he was given a good pair of binoculars. Later, when he wanted to sketch birds and animals, he was sent to spend some summer months in Nashville with a family his mother knew and was given watercolor lessons from Sister Mary Luke at the Convent of Saint Cecilia.

Other delightful activities of childhood brought forth different types of equipment. A rock collection begun and later abandoned set the ground for a book on geology. His parents also provided a chemistry set, a homemade radio set (that never worked, he admitted) and manuals on electricity and the Morse code.

Summers were spent with Robert Penn's grandfather Gabriel Thomas Penn on his farm near Cerulean Springs, Kentucky. A Confederate captain, the grandfather told Robert Penn stories of his rides with Nathan Bedford Forrest during the war and engaged the boy's interest in history with stories of Napoleon. He also quoted Byron, Scott and Romantic poetry, leading his daughters to call him "visionary" (by which they meant impractical) and Robert Penn to feel that his grandfather was almost larger than life. Grandfather Penn is credited along with Rob'Penn's parents with engendering in him a love for the spoken and written word.

The early life of his father seemed to hold a fascination for Robert Penn after Robert Franklin Warren died just before his eighty-sixth birthday. His father had spent a number of years in Clarksville, Tennessee, around 1890, when he was described in a newspaper as a "promising young man" after he was involved in an escape from a deadly tornado and was written up. (Robert Penn was able to see a yellowed copy of the paper many years later but was not sure whether the paper was from Louisville or Nashville.)

Robert Penn was never sure where his father had worked when he first moved to Clarksville but believed he had a job on the Cumberland River. His father eventually came into a good job probably because, although he probably had no more than a sixth-grade education, he began collecting books and reading them as a young man. He even engaged a Greek tutor and attempted to learn the language. In later years, Robert Penn was especially heartened that he still owned his father's Greek grammar and dictionary.

Robert Penn also retained his mother's set of Shakespeare's plays that he described as "well-thumbed, multivolumed" and "green-backed."

Robert Penn discovered a book, *The Poets of America*, one day when he was about eleven or twelve. The book fell open to a page at the top of which was the name of Robert Franklin Warren followed by several poems that he had written. There was also a photograph of Robert Penn's father from when he was about twenty-two or twenty-three. When his father came home, after

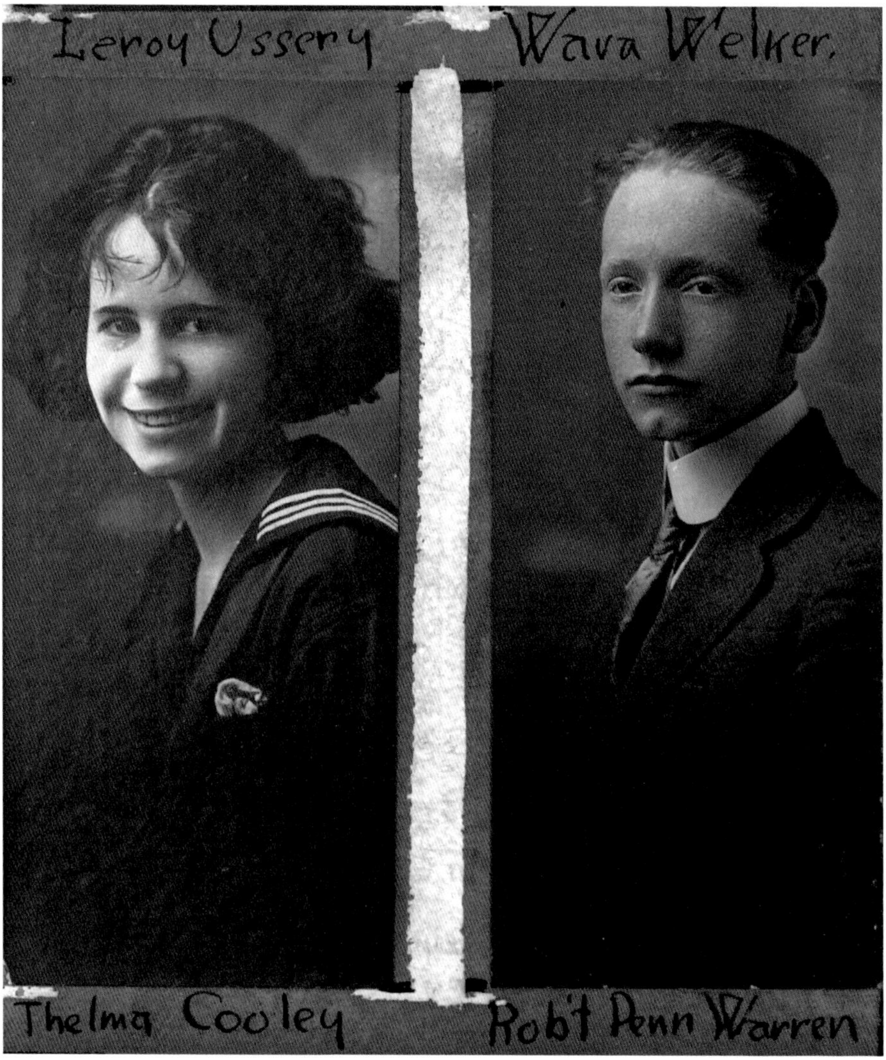


Robert Penn Warren's Clarksville High School graduation picture. *Robert Penn Warren Collection, Felix G. Woodward Library, Austin Peay State University.*

an impatient period of eager waiting on Robert Penn's part, Robert Penn showed the book to his father, who promptly looked at it, said nothing and took it to a hiding place where it was never to be seen again. Many years later, his sister, Mary, revealed that she had found the book and had "stolen" it. It appeared that the book was printed by a "vanity" press, and their father had not been proud of the fact.

When their father was in his seventies, he sent in a letter to Robert Penn a yellowed piece of paper with one of his poems on it signed "R.F.W." and typed the instructions, "Do not answer" at the bottom.

On April 9, 1984, Robert Penn Warren was asked to speak at the bicentennial of Austin Peay State University. Fortunately, that speech was recorded and is now located on tape both in the Felix G. Woodward Library at APSU and in Emory University's library.

In the speech, he describes (as he does in *A Portrait of a Father*) watching his father shave with a straight razor and hearing its "whack! whack!" After this procedure, Robert Franklin Warren would utter phrases that he told Robert Penn were in Greek. Robert Penn claimed that he believed, when still a little boy, that all people in Clarksville spoke Greek.

## CLARKSVILLE HIGH SCHOOL

*And I couldn't get in Vanderbilt because I was not old enough, so I had the good sense—or the good luck—to go to a very good high school in Clarksville the next year while waiting for my sixteenth year to go to Vanderbilt.*
*Robert Penn Warren*

Robert Penn Warren also spoke of riding the train to Clarksville when he was a "man" of fifteen to attend Clarksville High School during the bicentennial speech. In *A Portrait of a Father*, he tells that during that year, he stayed with a family who were friends with his parents during the week and went home for the weekend. He said that he was not too closely supervised and was only doing "what boys do" at the time, but he felt that he was truly entering manhood.

In the Felix G. Woodward Library at APSU hangs a class picture of Clarksville High School 1920–21. A very young-looking Robert Penn Warren has his picture there beside an oil portrait that was painted years later when he had become the only person to win a Pulitzer Prize for fiction and two Pulitzer Prizes for poetry.

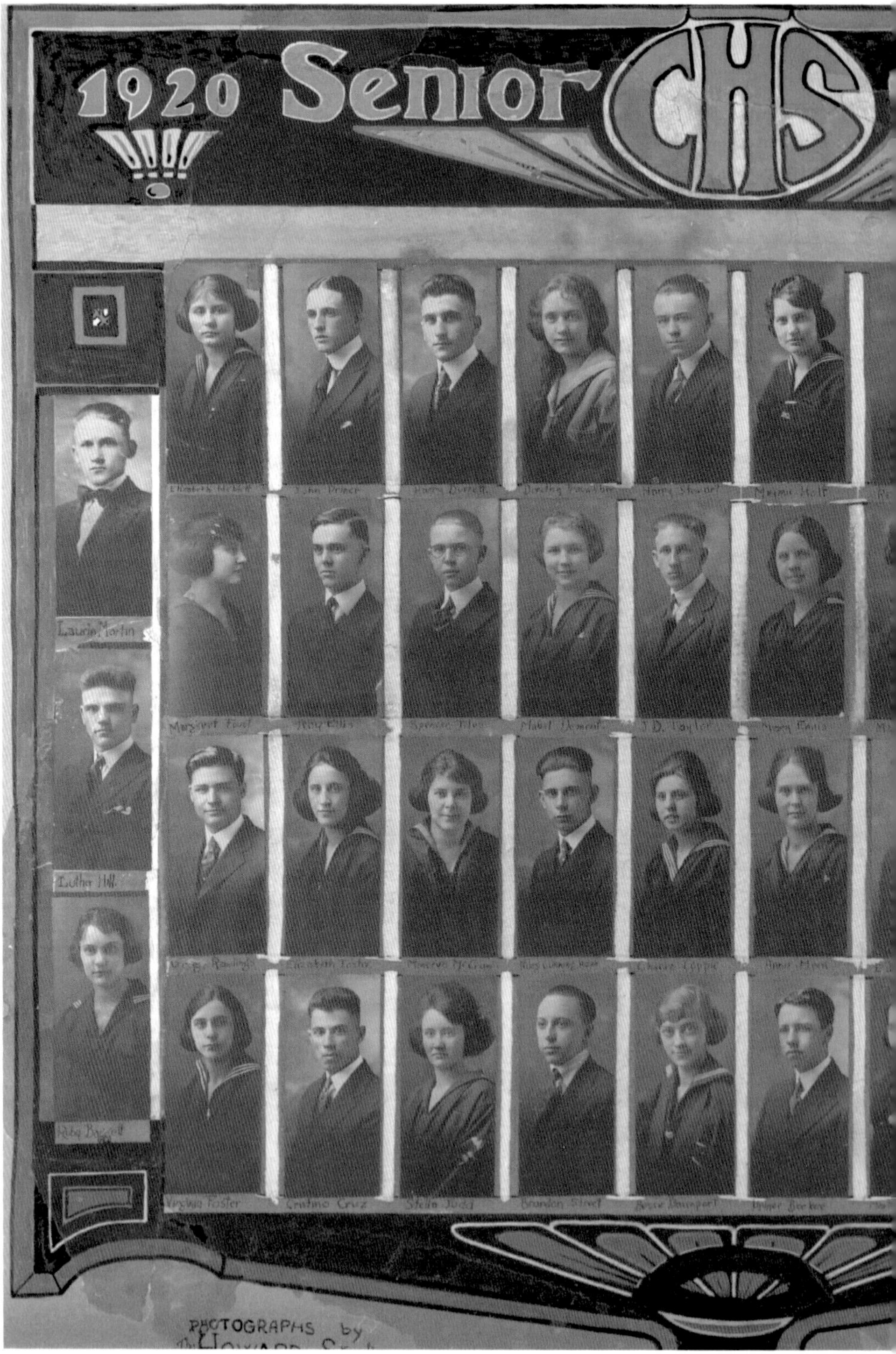
1920 Senior
CHS
Laurie Martin
Luther Hill
PHOTOGRAPHS by

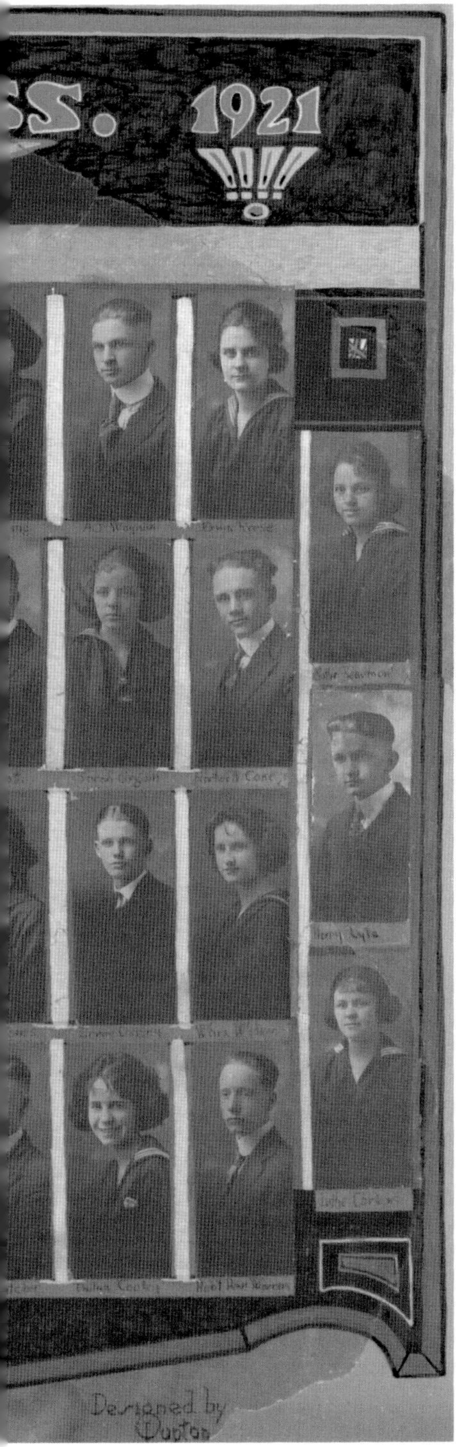


From 1917 until 1933, my paternal great-grandfather, Albert Wayne Jobe, served as superintendent of schools for Montgomery County. C.H. Moore was principal of Clarksville High School during the year that Robert Penn Warren was a student there (1921–21). These two men would most likely have been on the stage when Robert Penn Warren received his diploma.

The *Purple and Gold*, a literary monthly for students at Clarksville High School, featured a story, an essay and a short vignette by Robert Penn Warren. Remaining copies of the small magazine reveal "Munk" in the February 1921 issue of the *Purple and Gold* and "The Dream of a Driller" and "Senior Creed" in the April 1921 issue. (Robert Penn Warren signed a copy of "Munk" on April 9, 1984, when he returned to Clarksville. It is now located in Special Collections at the Felix G. Woodward Library.)

The ambitions of Robert Penn Warren when he entered Clarksville High School, having finished the Guthrie School the previous year, were those formed when he saw the young son of a friend of his mother exit a train in Guthrie. The young man had just graduated from the United States Naval Academy at Annapolis and was wearing his summer white dress uniform that sported brass buttons and epaulets.

Clarksville High School graduates, 1921. Robert Penn Warren is in the bottom right corner. *Robert Penn Warren Collection, Felix G. Woodward Library, Austin Peay State University.*

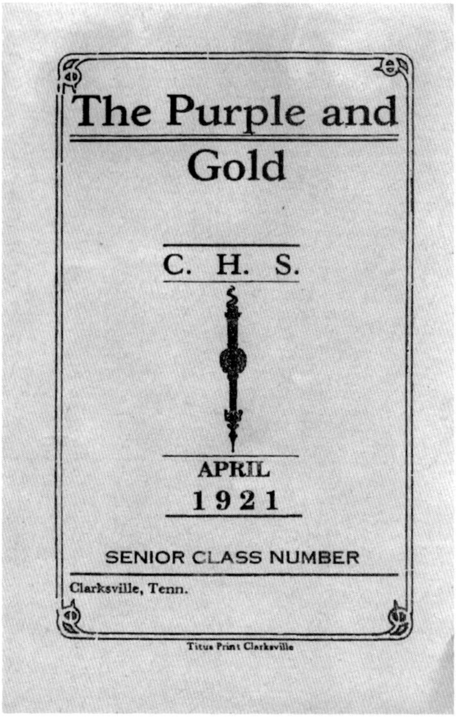
The Purple and Gold

C. H. S.

APRIL 1921

SENIOR CLASS NUMBER

Clarksville, Tenn.

Titus Print Clarksville

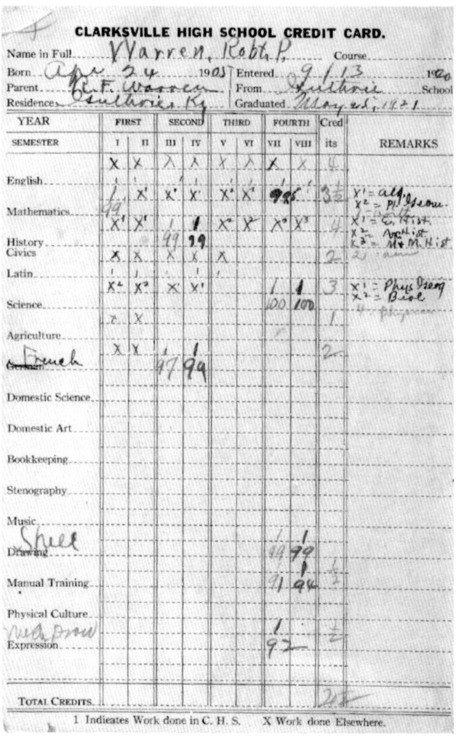
CLARKSVILLE HIGH SCHOOL CREDIT CARD.

Name in Full Warren, Robt. P. Course

Born Apr. 24 1905 Entered 9/13 1920

Parent R.F. Warren From Guthrie School

Residence Guthrie, Ky. Graduated May 26, 1921

YEAR: FIRST, SECOND, THIRD, FOURTH, Credits, REMARKS

English, Mathematics, History, Civics, Latin, Science, Agriculture, French, Domestic Science, Domestic Art, Bookkeeping, Stenography, Music, Drawing, Manual Training, Physical Culture, Expression

TOTAL CREDITS

1 Indicates Work done in C. H. S. X Work done Elsewhere.

Giving Robert Penn a "manly handshake" after having kissed his mother, the young man made such an impression on Robert Penn that he was determined from then on to go to the U.S. Naval Academy.

Although his father strongly desired that Robert Penn would become an attorney, Robert Penn stuck to his desire to make the navy his career. Robert Franklin made arrangements with their congressman, R.Y. Thomas, for Robert Penn to be appointed to Annapolis.

For six weeks during the summer of 1921, Robert Penn Warren attended Citizens Military Training Corps at Fort Knox, Kentucky. During that time, his first poem, "Prophecy," was published in the *Messkit*.

The summer after Robert Penn Warren graduated from Clarksville High School changed those plans forever. His younger brother, Thomas, was, for some unknown reason, throwing objects. In some descriptions, the objects are described as "stones," and in others,

*Top*: The *Purple and Gold* cover, April 1921. *Robert Penn Warren Collection, Felix G. Woodward Library, Austin Peay State University.*

*Bottom*: Robert Penn Warren's report card. *Robert Penn Warren Collection, Felix G. Woodward Library, Austin Peay State University.*

they are "chunks of coal." Whichever is true, one landed in Robert Penn's left eye and caused that eye to have to be removed. Thus, he could not pass the physical to go to the Naval Academy and, consequently, entered Vanderbilt University in the fall of 1921 at the ripe age of sixteen.

## VANDERBILT

*For this was the time of the Fugitives at Vanderbilt, a group of poets and arguers—including John Crowe Ransom, Donald Davidson, Allen Tate, Merrill Moore—and I imagine that more of my education came from those sessions than from the classroom.*
*Robert Penn Warren*

The loss of Robert Penn's eye has not been a subject discussed at length by many of those who have written about his life, yet the man himself admitted to feeling "maimed" and "disqualified for life" as a result of this injury. Furthermore, because one side of the brain controls the opposite side of the body, the brain has a significant adjustment period for an injury of this kind. The loss of peripheral vision and lack of depth perception is an ever-present risk for further injury. Losing an eye is not a minor annoyance to be brushed aside as being insignificant. It is a life-changing event.

Many years later, in "Red-Tailed Hawk and Pyre of Youth," he describes finding a hawk that is missing not only one leg but also one eye and poignantly says, "And I reckoned/I knew how it felt with one gone."

During his years at Vanderbilt, Robert Penn had bouts of depression brought on by having been told that it was possible that he would lose sight in his other eye through "sympathetic blindness." At one point in 1924, he even attempted suicide, but he was able to overcome his depression because his sight did not fail.

Entering Vanderbilt University in Nashville after his chance at a naval career was dashed, Robert Penn's original major was chemistry, but after one semester in the classroom of John Crowe Ransom, a renowned writer, his fate was sealed, as the focus of the rest of his life became literature.

Years later, in an interview in the March 12, 1977 *National Observer*, he remarked, "I've been to a lot of places and done a lot of things, but writing was always first. It's a kind of pain I can't do without." Robert Penn Warren came to see himself first as a poet and second as a novelist and critic.

Robert Penn Warren's life at Vanderbilt was nothing short of remarkable. He became the youngest member of a group called the Fugitives (the name of their literary magazine). The original members of the group were John Crowe Ransom, Donald Davidson, Allen Tate, Alec Stevenson, Stanley Johnson, Walter Clyde Curry and Sidney Hirsch. The group eventually included Merrill Moore, James M. Frank, William Yandell Elliott, Jesse and Ridley Wills, William Frierson, Andrew Lytle, Alfred Starr, Laura Riding and, of course, Robert Penn Warren, whom his friends began to call "Red" (because of his red hair).

The Fugitives usually met together at the home of James Frank or in Ransom's or Curry's office, though they used other locations at times. Their magazine, the *Fugitive*, eventually published twenty-three of Red's poems but ceased publication after only three and a half years. This was not a group under the wings of Vanderbilt University but a group of young men who got together to discuss ideas and create what they called the "New Criticism." New Criticism focused on close reading of a literary work in order to determine cultural values through careful attention to language with a focus on problems of interpreting individual texts.

The poetry of the Fugitives expressed their desire to correct the way people saw the South. The immense contributions of four of these poets impacted literature and redefined Southern poetry forever.

Two of Red's stories appeared in the March 1925 issue of the *Fugitive* (which sold for twenty-five cents): "Iron Beach" and "The Mirror."

The Agrarians were an additional group at Vanderbilt that evolved from the Fugitives movement. They were also called the Twelve Southerners, the Vanderbilt Agrarians, the Nashville Agrarians, the Tennessee Agrarians and the Fugitive Agrarians.

*I'll Take My Stand: The South and the Agrarian Tradition by Twelve Southerners (1930)* was the name of a collection of essays by the group encouraging the return to a rural South as opposed to Northern industrialization, capitalism and scientific basis for interaction. The Agrarians did not believe that progress was served through factory labor and the rise of urbanization. Their theories also supported a cultural elite brought about through struggle. The group included not only Warren, Davidson, Ransom and Tate but also John Gould Fletcher, Henry Blue Kline, Lyle Hicks Lanier, Andrew Nelson Lytle, Herman Clarence Nixon, Frank Lawrence Owsley, John Donald Wade and Stark Young.

These men became throughout the 1920s and '30s the base members of a movement now termed the "Southern Renaissance." Literature in the

South had previously focused primarily on historical romances mainly about what was termed the "Lost Cause" of the Confederacy following the end of the War Between the States (also known as "the Recent Unpleasantness" by certain Southerners). These writers from Vanderbilt, along with William Faulkner, Katherine Anne Porter, Caroline Gordon, Tennessee Williams, and Elizabeth Madox Roberts, changed the course of Southern literature to focus on the conflicted Southern conscience concerning racial attitudes, conservative culture and the burden of history following the war.

## Beyond Tennessee

*You fight your battles one by one and do the best you can.*
*Robert Penn Warren*

Finishing Vanderbilt *summa cum laude*, Phi Beta Kappa and with the Founders' Medal for his bachelor of arts degree, Robert Penn Warren went on to the University of California, where he received a master's degree in 1927. He then studied at Yale University from 1927 to 1928 and became a Rhodes Scholar at the University of Oxford, where he received a bachelor of letters in 1930.

Red Warren was only twenty-four when he wrote *John Brown: The Making of a Martyr*. It was published during his years at Oxford. Also while at Oxford, he met Cleanth Brooks, also a Rhodes Scholar; they later wrote textbooks that had a major impact on the study of literature.

The life and career of Robert Penn Warren has been documented through scores of volumes written by historians and experts in literature, both during his life and since his death. Near the end of his life, Warren worked with Joseph Blotner, who has written the definitive biography *Robert Penn Warren*; its five hundred pages give intimate details of Warren's life that anyone who loves Warren's work should experience.

His writing, discussed only briefly here, included ten books of fiction, seventeen volumes of poetry, two books of short stories, twelve books of nonfiction, several textbooks, three books for children, one play and six selections of essays. Warren's prodigious works came from his work ethic, which was described by Ralph McGill who lived next door to him one summer in the Vanderbilt dormitories. McGill said in "Formaldehyde and Poetry" (quoted in *Literary Nashville*) that "his [Warren's] light always was burning, no matter how late the hour. I marveled then at his discipline and have never ceased to do so."

When Warren left Oxford, he became an assistant professor of English at Southwestern College in Memphis in 1930. He then served as assistant professor of English at Vanderbilt from 1931 to 1934. In 1934, he moved to Louisiana State University, again as assistant professor of English but was promoted to associate professor in 1936.

At LSU, Red Warren published *Thirty-Six Poems* in 1935. That same year was the date of the founding of the *Southern Review* with Charles W. Pipkin as editor, Cleanth Brooks and Robert Penn Warren as managing editors and Albert Erskine as business manager.

Thomas H. Landess, on May 17, 2011, recalled that Governor Huey Long was responsible for the initiation of the *Southern Review*, but the official version reads a bit differently. On the LSU website, in an article entitled "The Southern Review Celebrates 75 Years of Literary Excellence," the person who is identified as having the idea for the journal is "the president of Louisiana State University, James Monroe Smith," and the people in the black Cadillac where it was initially discussed are Red Warren, Mrs. Warren and Albert Erskine.

Whoever was responsible, the *Southern Review* became one of the foremost cultural and literary quarterlies in the United States. Authors such as Eudora Welty, Katherine Anne Porter, Allan Tate and scores of others were published in it until 1942, when it suspended publication after twenty-eight issues. Publication began again in 1965 and continues today. The list of Nobel Laureates, Pulitzer Prize winners, National Book Award winners and other prize winners who have published in the *Southern Review* is extensive.

In 1936, Robert Penn Warren won the Helen Haire Levinson Prize for Poetry, and in 1936, 1937 and 1938, he won the Caroline Sinkler Prize for Poetry of South Carolina.

With Cleanth Brooks, Warren wrote *An Approach to Literature*, *Understanding Poetry*, *Understanding Fiction* and *Modern Rhetoric, with Readings*. These books influenced the study of writing for thousands, perhaps millions, of students in the following years.

In 1939, Robert Penn Warren not only published *Night Rider* but also won the first of his two Guggenheim Fellowships, the second being in 1947–48. After the *Southern Review* ceased publication in 1942, Warren moved to the University of Minnesota as a professor of English.

In 1942, he received the Poet of the Month Award for "Eleven Poems on the Same Theme." In 1943, he won the Shelly Memorial Award, and in

1944, he became the second occupant of the Chair of Poetry at the Library of Congress.

In 1943, *At Heaven's Gate* appeared. In 1944, *Selected Poems, 1923–1943* was published, and Warren became Consultant of Poetry for the Library of Congress. *Blackberry Winter*, a collection of short stories, was published in 1946.

The momentous publication of *All the King's Men*, for which Warren won his first Pulitzer Prize, also occurred in 1946. Originally based on a verse play called *Proud Flesh* that Warren began work on in 1936, this book is a landmark in American literature as Willie Stark (supposedly based on Huey Long, although Warren later jokingly claimed the character was based on Julius Caesar) takes his place as an unforgettable character. The book was the talk of the country and eventually, in 1949, was made into a movie that won three Oscars for Best Picture, Best Actor (Broderick Crawford) and Best Supporting Actress (Mercedes McCambridge).

In 1947, Warren won the Southern Author's Award, which was sponsored by the Southern Women's National Democratic Organization.

Also in 1947 came the publication of *The Circus in the Attic and Other Stories* followed by his receiving the Robert Meltzer Award of the Screen Writers' Guild for *All the King's Men* and an honorary doctorate of letters from the University of Louisville.

In 1950, he attained membership in the National Institute of Arts and Letters, became Chancellor of the American Academy of Poets and received a Distinguished Alumnus Award from Vanderbilt University.

*World Enough and Time* was published in 1950. Also in 1950, Warren left the University of Minnesota to move to Yale University, where he was professor of playwriting.

During this time, Warren's personal life involved a divorce from his first wife, Emma Cinina Brescia Warren, whom he had secretly married in 1925 after he returned from England. Her emotional instability became almost legendary. Their divorce was final on June 28, 1951, after Emma suffered a breakdown and Red was advised by her psychiatrist to end the marriage. It was reported that Warren took an apartment across the street from her at first in order to make certain she was all right. He had met her at Vanderbilt. They had no children. It was reported in several descriptions that their marriage was full of drama as Emma was reported to be prone to loud tantrums and once even tossed furniture at their hostess. Her mental illness and jealousy of Warren's success have been documented in his biography by Joseph Blotner.

On December 7, 1952, he married Eleanor Clark. This marriage produced two children, Rosanna Phelps Warren and Gabriel Penn

Warren. By all reports, the marriage gave Red Warren the happiest days of his life.

After publishing verse for several years, Warren produced *Brother to Dragons: A Tale in Verse and Voices* in 1953 followed by *Segregation: The Inner Conflict in the South* in 1956 and *Promises, Poems 1954–56* in 1957, which won the Pulitzer Prize. *Band of Angels*, *Remember the Alamo*, *The Gods of Mount Olympus* and *How Texas Won Her Freedom* (the last three are children's books) were his next offerings. *The Cave* was published in 1959, the year that Warren was elected to the American Academy of Arts and Letters.

In 1960, Warren became professor of English at Yale. The 1960s saw a prolific period with the following publications: *You, Emperors, and Others: Poems* (1960); *Wilderness: A Tale of the Civil War* (1961); *Flood: A Romance of Our Time* (1964); *Who Speaks for the Negro?* (1965); *Selected Poems: New and Old* (1966), which won the Bollinger Prize in Poetry; *Incarnations: Poems 1966–1968* (1968); *The Circus in the Attic and other Stories* (1968); and *Audubon: A Vision (1969)*, winning the National Medal for Literature and the Van Wyck Brooks Award.

The 1970s were equally prolific with *Selected Poems of Herman Melville: A Reader's Edition* (1970); *Meet Me in the Green Glen* (1971); *Homage to Theodore Dreiser: On the Centennial of His Birth* (1971); *John Greenleaf Whittier's Poetry: An Appraisal and a Selection* (1971); *Or Else: Poem/Poems 1968–1974* (1974); *Selected Poems: 1923–1975* (1976); and *Now and Then: Poems 1976-1978* (1978), which won his second Pulitzer Prize for Poetry. *Brother to Dragons: A New Version* was published in 1979.

In 1973, Warren retired from Yale University.

*American Literature: The Makers and the Making* was published with Cleanth Brooks and R.W.B. Lewis as coauthors in 1974.

In "retirement," Robert Penn Warren witnessed the publication of *Robert Penn Warren Talking: Interviews 1950–1978* and *Being Here: Poetry 1977-1980.* Then, in 1981 came *Jefferson Davis Gets His Citizenship Back.* (Jefferson Davis was born in Todd County, Kentucky, the same county in which Guthrie is located.) *Chief Joseph of the Nez Perce* (1983) was followed by *New and Selected Poems: 1923–1985* (1985).

The Presidential Medal of Freedom was presented to Robert Penn Warren by President Jimmy Carter on June 8, 1980. Warren was selected as a MacArthur Fellow in 1981, and on February 26, 1986, librarian of Congress Daniel J. Boorstin announced the appointment of Robert Penn Warren as the first Poet Laureate Consultant in Poetry. His biography of his father, *Portrait of a Father*, was published in 1988.

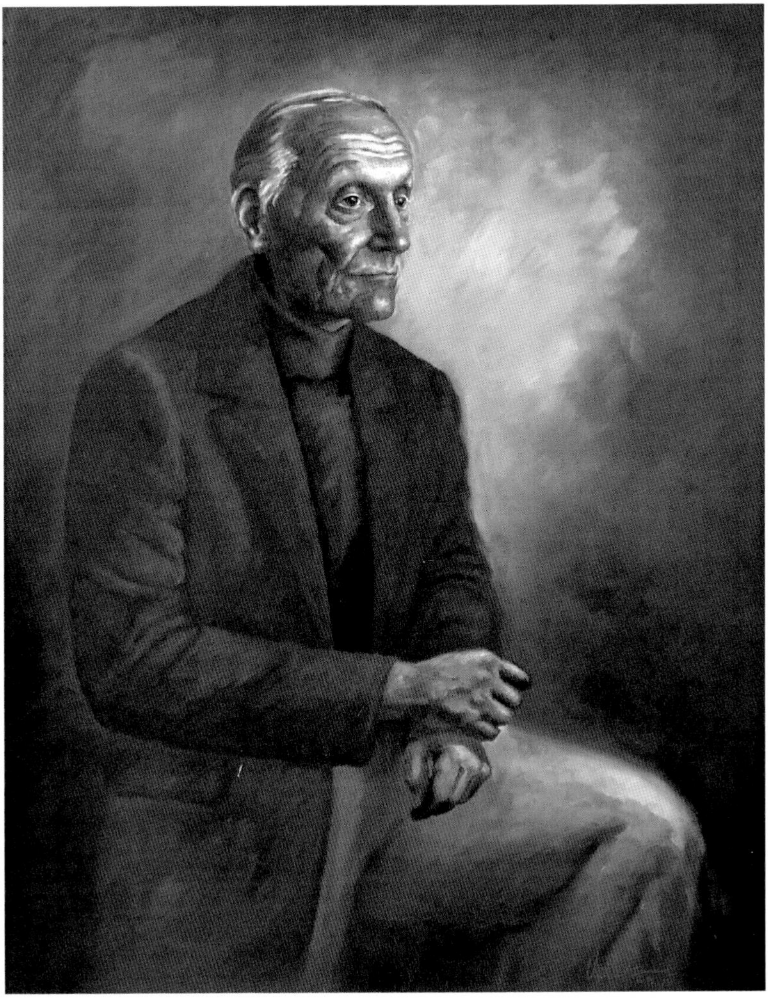

Portrait of Robert Penn Warren. *Gift of Patricia and Howard Winn to Felix G. Woodward Library, Austin Peay State University.*

Robert Penn Warren died of bone cancer on September 15, 1989, at his summer home in Stratton, Vermont. Warren's death occurred when he was eighty-four and was a resident of Fairfield, Connecticut. The *New York Times* reported that he was survived by his wife; his sister, Mary Barber of Maysville, Kentucky; his daughter, Rosanna Scully of Needham, Massachusetts; his son, Gabriel, of Washington County, Rhode Island; and three grandchildren. Warren is buried in Stratton, but as he requested, a memorial marker is located in the Warren family gravesite in Guthrie, Kentucky.

A commemorative stamp was issued by the U.S. Post Office in April 2005, on the one-hundredth anniversary of Robert Penn Warren's birth.

Papers of Robert Penn Warren can be located at the libraries of Yale and Emory Universities and at the Felix G. Woodward Library of Austin Peay State University.

*Life is a process of trial and error about our own values.*

*Robert Penn Warren*

## Warren's Tennessee Legacy

The Robert Penn Warren Center for the Humanities is sponsored by the College of Arts and Sciences at Vanderbilt University. Established for interdisciplinary research and study of natural sciences, social sciences and humanities, it was funded by a $480,000 grant from the National Endowment for the Humanities. Professors such as A. Scott Pearson, surgeon and author of medical mystery novels, meet with other faculty members from various disciplines to learn and study with each other.

The old Clarksville High School, constructed in 1906, was made into sixty-five loft-style apartments now called the Penn Warren Apartments.

The Warren-Brooks Award was established to honor the innovative critical interpretation of literature offered by Robert Penn Warren and Cleanth Brooks and to celebrate the continuation of such achievement. It is awarded for outstanding literary criticism originally published in English in the United States and is given in those years when a book, or other worthy publication, appears that exemplifies the Warren-Brooks effort in spirit, scope and integrity. The recipient receives a $1,000 check and a certificate of recognition. Arrangements for the recipient include an expenses-paid trip to Western Kentucky University in Bowling Green, Kentucky, to receive the award.

Locations in Clarksville, Tennessee, where information about Robert Penn Warren is found include the Felix G. Woodward Library at Austin Peay State University, the County Archives, the Montgomery County Library and the Historical Society. The Customs House Museum is also a location of interest.

The Robert Penn Warren Birthplace Museum (where he was born but did not live very long) is located in Guthrie, Kentucky, on the corner of Cherry and Third Streets. It is open Tuesday through Sunday with hours

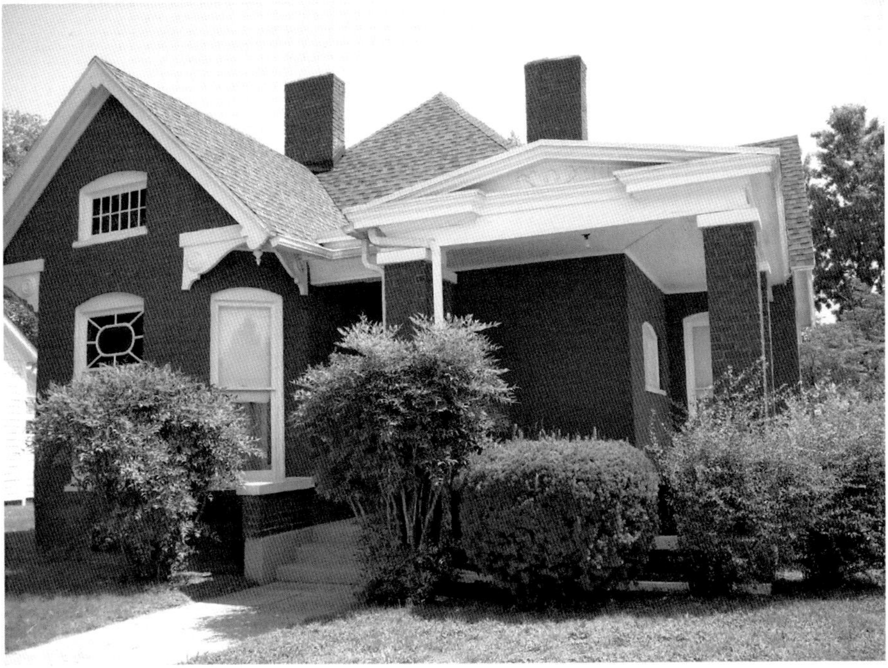

Robert Penn Warren birthplace, Guthrie, Kentucky. *Sue Freeman Culverhouse.*

listed at www.robertpennwarren.com/birthpla.htm. The telephone number is 270-483-2683. Docents can give the visitor extensive information about the life of Robert Penn Warren, and the museum has a significant selection of his books for sale. The small house has a large variety of mementos from the life of Robert Penn Warren, including pictures of his family, well-known photographs from throughout his life (a large portrait by Annie Leibowitz shows him without a shirt and, according to a docent at the museum, was thoroughly disliked by one of his wives) and furniture of the period. The museum is visited by people from all over the world.

The Robert Penn Warren Circle meets each year during April in Bowling Green, Kentucky, and later at Austin Peay State University. A luncheon in Guthrie, Kentucky, occurs after these meetings with additional lectures in the afternoon. Extensive information on the life and work of Robert Penn Warren is located at the group's website, www.robertpennwarren.com. In 2013, a tree was planted in memory of Warren across the street from the Birthplace Museum with attendees reading selections from his poetry.

CHAPTER TWO

# PETER MATTHEW HILLSMAN TAYLOR AND HIS WIFE, POET ELEANOR ROSS TAYLOR

*I feel identified with Tennessee, North Carolina, and the Upper South. I feel that it's a part of me and that I'm a part of it.*
*Peter Taylor*

On January 8, 1917, a son was born to Matthew Hillsman "Red" Taylor of football fame and Katherine Baird (Taylor) Taylor. The fourth child of this marriage, he was named Matthew Hillsman Taylor Jr. but called "Pete" because of baby talk used for "sweet." Throughout his life, he was called Pete by his family. Years later, he wrote as Peter Taylor, the name by which he is known throughout the world.

Peter Taylor is not a household name, but in the literary world, he is a giant. Primarily known for his short stories, of which he was a master, he also wrote novels and plays. He won the Pulitzer Prize for *A Summons to Memphis* in 1987 after struggling for a great deal of his life to decide whether or not he could even write a novel.

The life of Peter Taylor, itself, is as interesting as the plot of any novel, beginning with the history of his family, the early days mainly reported by Hubert H. McAlexander in his biography *Peter Taylor: A Writer's Life*. McAlexander also compiled an extensive collection of discussions with Taylor and numerous other writers, *Conversations with Peter Taylor*, that provides insight into Taylor's feelings on many subjects.

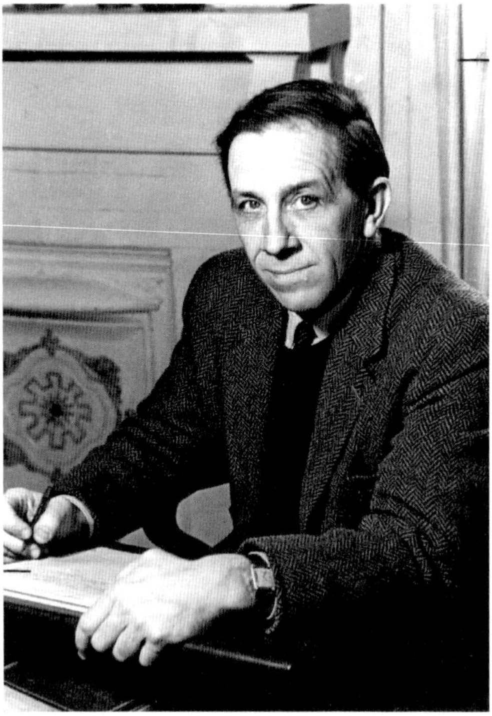

Peter Taylor. *Albert and Shirley Small Special Collections Library, University of Virginia.*

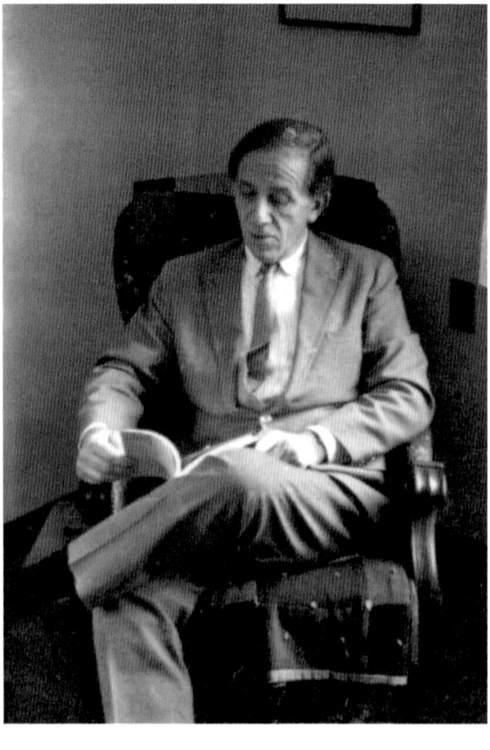

Peter Taylor. *Albert and Shirley Small Special Collections Library, University of Virginia.*

## Family Background

Matthew Hillsman "Red" Taylor, Peter's father, was the son of Colonel Robert Zachary Taylor, a respected lawyer and pillar of the Baptist Church, from which Red was kicked out for drinking, dancing and card playing. Red Taylor was a star football player, first at the University of Tennessee in Knoxville and later—incurring his own father's wrath for changing schools—at Vanderbilt University in Nashville. After obtaining a law degree, Red returned to Trenton, Tennessee, to join his father's law practice and then became the youngest Speaker of the Tennessee House of Representatives.

Katherine Taylor was a member of a different Taylor family from Red's. Her father was Robert Love Taylor who was so loved by people who knew him that he was referred to as "Our Bob." Three times governor of Tennessee in nonconsecutive terms and later a senator for six years, Bob Taylor also gained fame during an election known in Tennessee as the War of the Roses. A Democrat from an old Whig-Republican district, he ran in 1886 against his own brother, Alf, a Republican. They would "politic" against each other during the day, play their fiddles for the crowds and, on many occasions, sleep in the same bed that night. Close friends, the two men were also running against their father, Reverend Nathaniel Taylor, the Prohibition candidate who did not even campaign. "Our Bob" won. Much later, in the 1920s, Alf also became governor when he was in his seventies.

When Robert Love Taylor died suddenly while serving in the Senate, the *New York Times* wrote in his obituary that he was probably the only man in the political arena who was successful for the sole reason that people loved him. His body was carried back to Tennessee on a train; he then lay in state in the capitol in Nashville for the crowds of mourners to view. Then, the train carried him through Tennessee to Knoxville, where he was buried. Peter Taylor's last book, *In the Tennessee Country*, describes his trip on the train when he was four years old. The book itself is a study in how an author takes family stories and creates fiction in the highest sense.

Robert Love Taylor was married three times. His first wife, Sally Baird of Asheville, North Carolina, was considered the love of his life. She was mother to his five children. Their daughter, Katherine Baird Taylor, the mother of Peter Taylor, lost her mother when she was quite young. Her father married briefly the daughter of the governor of Alabama and, in later life, married Mamie Love St. John, a cousin, in a marriage of convenience.

Katherine—or "Kate," as she was called—moved around a great deal to live with her Baird relatives and with one of her aunts, Mrs. Alf Taylor in East Tennessee; she was eventually educated at Belmont College in Nashville. She was quite musical and could play both the piano and banjo as she sang. She was a gifted storyteller, as were many of Peter's relatives.

Red Taylor's father, Robert Zachary Taylor, was a private under Nathan Bedford Forrest during the War Between the States. At Confederate reunions, he was promoted to "colonel." In addition to his law practice, he had farming, business and political interests.

In October 1908, Colonel Taylor was kidnapped along with his law partner, Captain Quentin Rankin. They were in the Walnut Log Hotel in Samburg at the edge of Reelfoot Lake when Night Riders took them into custody. While the hooded men were hanging Rankin, Taylor dived into the lake and escaped. He was found, dazed, wandering in the swamp. The governor called out the militia to capture the Night Riders, and it was successful. Peter Taylor remembered all his life the clothes that had belonged to Rankin and were kept on top of his grandfather's wardrobe. This episode also found its way into Peter's writing.

## Early Childhood

*Any society that doesn't have the family as a basic cultural and economic unit is a barbarian dunghill.*
*Peter Taylor*

Red Taylor and Katherine Taylor were married in Nashville on January 8, 1908. Moving to Trenton, Tennessee, Red joined his father's law firm. In October 1910, Sally Baird Taylor was born, followed in the summer of 1912 by the birth of Mettie Ivie Taylor. The first son, Robert Love Taylor, was born in the spring of 1915, followed by the youngest son, who would gain fame as one of the greatest short story writers, (Peter) Matthew Hillsman Taylor Jr. Peter's mother said that some of her happiest years were the first years of her marriage when she lived in Trenton, where Red's family welcomed and loved her.

## Nashville Years

In 1915, Hillsman "Red" Taylor was elected as attorney general of the Seventy-third Judicial District of Tennessee. In 1921, he moved his family to Nashville, as he became the corporation lawyer for Rogers Caldwell, the greatest financier in the South at the time. Caldwell and Taylor were to become best friends.

The move from Trenton to Nashville involved a caravan of two vehicles with parents, children, pets and servants riding together. They arrived at nearly midnight, a journey of about 150 miles, because of nine flat tires (not an uncommon event in the early days of automobiles). Their first home was Traveller's Rest, built by John Overton, who was the law partner and business associate of Andrew Jackson. This house was rented while their permanent residence was under repair. The "Claiborne House" on Hogan Lane was near Oak Hill, the residence of Caldwell. The children called it "the House of Seven Gables" and seemed to have had an idyllic time there. The girls went to Ward-Belmont College, and the boys rode their ponies to Robertson Academy.

## On to St. Louis

*According to one of my aunts, the Taylors were originally Taliaferros* [pronounced Tolliver]. *She didn't want anyone to think that we had come from someone who made clothes.*
*Peter Taylor*

After two years, Caldwell moved the Taylors to St. Louis, where Hillsman could be put in charge of Cotton States Insurance Company. After purchasing the Missouri State Life Insurance Company, Caldwell and Company also purchased a three-story house with a basement on Washington Terrace that would not only house the insurance firm but also the Taylor family. The third floor had a ballroom, where Peter was later to hold his own tea dance. Hillsman arranged that his butler, chauffeur and cook were all African Americans from Trenton. The girls were sent to the Mary Institute and the boys to Miss Rossman's School.

Governor Alf Taylor came to St. Louis to speak at the Jackson Day celebration. Peter loved to hear his uncle's stories and used some of them in his book *In the Tennessee Country*.

Peter won the sixth grade literary prize with his essay on the escape of his grandfather from the Night Riders. He also wrote plays that were performed in the family ballroom by his friends.

On October 9, 1930, Peter's older sister Sally was presented to society as a maid of honor at the Fifty-first Veiled Prophet's Ball, the ultimate social event in St. Louis. Even after the crash in 1929, the Taylors continued to live as if no financial crisis had affected them. Both girls were sent to Europe to tour for the summer.

On November 14, 1930, Caldwell and Company announced insolvency and went into receivership. In April 1931, Caldwell was indicted in Kentucky for fraud in the BancoKy merger. That summer, the stock in Missouri State Life Insurance began to fall. Nevertheless, on October 7, 1931, Mettie Taylor had her debut in St. Louis. At age forty-seven, Hillsman Taylor had to resign as president of the life insurance company on December 1, 1931, in spite of his not having had knowledge of the Caldwell Company's gambling with the money of other people. Caldwell did not come to St. Louis to defend his friend, and from that day on, Hillsman refused to allow anyone in his household to speak Caldwell's name. (Many years later, the two men were reconciled when they encountered each other in Monteagle.)

On January 1, 1932, the Taylors moved to an apartment on Waterman Avenue in St. Louis. The furnishings of the mansion on Washington Terrace were auctioned, and a few years later, the house was razed leaving only a hole where the basement had been.

## Memphis Bound

*My writing is a byproduct of my efforts to understand my life; that's what it comes to.*
Peter Taylor

At first, it appeared that the family might have to move back to Trenton so that Hillsman could rejoin his father's law firm, but in October 1932, he joined a law firm in Memphis. Soon after they moved, the Taylors joined the Memphis Country Club and entered society in spite of their being in rather desperate financial straits. They were also listed in the first Memphis social register, as Peter entered the largest public school in Memphis, Central High School. Always friendly and gregarious, by the time he was a senior, he was editor of the school newspaper, for which he wrote a satirical column, Lord Chatterfill'd's Letters to His Sons, and the editorial page.

Both of Peter's sisters were married in their family home in Memphis in 1933. Mettie, the younger sister, married Duncan Dobson from St. Louis on April 18, 1933. Over the initial objections of her father, Sally married Millsaps Fitzhugh on October 14. Fitzhugh was an attorney who had been previously married to a dancer and had gone through a "lurid" public divorce that was followed in the newspapers. Although he was from a wealthy family and was well known in the Democratic Party, Fitzhugh was not considered a suitable husband for Sally by Hillsman, but she overruled her father ultimately. Fitzhugh had a four-year-old daughter at the time of the marriage; Peter was very fond of the little girl and of her father as well.

Peter began a lifelong interest in art during his high school years in Memphis and wanted to become an artist, much to the horror of his father. When Peter won a $2,000 scholarship (to be used at $500 a year) to Columbia University, awarded at his graduation in May 1935, he was dismayed that his father insisted that he could go only to Vanderbilt, where Hillsman planned for him to get a law degree. Feeling that his father would relent, Peter left for Europe on a merchant ship from New Orleans with his friend Jimmy Smithwick. They were surprised to learn that their voyage was not free—they would have to work their way over, which Peter did by waiting tables and cleaning rooms. After nine days in London, the boys returned to dock in Galveston and proceed home on the train.

When Hillsman was adamant that Peter could not go to Columbia, Peter balked on going to Vanderbilt and got a job working as an errand boy at the *Memphis Commercial Appeal*, but he was not happy with this situation. He eventually took some classes as a special student at Southwestern College (later Rhodes College); this was to change his life. There he met Allan Tate, whom Peter described throughout his life as the best teacher he ever had. Peter received an *A*+ on his paper based on a quotation from his maternal grandfather, Robert Love Taylor, "Speak not to me of the New South; there is only the Old South, risen, with the prints of the nails in her hands." Tate said on many occasions that after two weeks, he realized he could not teach Peter anything and asked him to leave the class. "The simple truth is that he did not need to know anything I could teach him. He had a perfection of style at the age of 18 I envied," Tate insisted.

Peter Taylor described Tate thus: "He gave all of us what was most significant in the world for us at the time. He inspired us with ideas concerning the importance of becoming a writer…One never again doubted what one's calling was."

Without Peter's knowledge, Tate was sending Peter's stories to Robert Penn Warren at the *Southern Review*.

This was the turning point in Peter Taylor's life.

## Education and the Writer's Life

Peter went on to Vanderbilt, where he studied under John Crowe Ransom and Donald Davidson. Peter's father was happy because he remembered when Ransom had arrived at Vanderbilt wearing knee breeches.

"Peter Hillsman Taylor" registered under this name at Vanderbilt, where Ransom was to encourage Taylor to write poetry rather than fiction. This year was in his father's eyes a failure because Peter's grades ended up placing him on probation at the end of the year. His courses were heavy with math, his weakest subject. Failing algebra the first semester and trigonometry in the second (plus botany and gym), Peter was called home to Memphis. He had made an *A* in his English course under Ransom, which was no mean feat. At Vanderbilt, he had met Randall Jarrell, a poet, essayist and novelist. A prodigy, Jarrell was by this time a celebrated writer.

Although the two stories that Tate sent Warren were rejected by the *Southern Review*, they were published in *River*, one in the first issue, along with a story by Eudora Welty. (In later years, Robert Penn Warren wrote the introduction to Taylor's first book, and in it, he said that he was sorry that he had rejected these stories. Peter claimed that he was grateful to Warren because it was the correct thing to do and praised Warren as a great friend and wonderful companion. He admired Warren for being truly Southern but feeling that he could criticize the South where necessary.)

Hearing that Ransom was acquiring scholarships to Kenyon College, where he was joining the faculty, Peter applied and was accepted. Entering in 1938, Peter Taylor began rejecting the name he was given at birth and his childhood nickname.

He roomed with Robert Traill Spence Lowell, called "Cal" (for Caligula because of his interest in Romans). Lowell and Taylor were to be lifelong friends in spite of the various breakdowns that Cal suffered. A brilliant poet who won two Pulitzer Prizes (1947 and 1974) and the National Book Award (1960) and was named the sixth Poet Laureate Consultant to the Library of

Congress (1947 to 1948), Lowell was described by Peter as having a terrible appearance but being so personable that he could command the attention of anyone he wanted to know. Taylor said that Cal rarely bathed or cut his hair, had shoe soles that flapped because they were not properly attached and had one decent suit that just hung in the closet. Lowell was brilliant intellectually and introduced Peter Taylor to a whole new world of literature.

Peter Taylor, in his story "1939," describes a trip the two took to New York to see two women, Jean Stafford (whom Lowell later married) and Virginia Jett. The trip was a disaster from every angle but became one of Taylor's best-known stories. Tate said that Peter should have used the real names, but Cal and Jean were horrified to see themselves in writing in spite of their having told Peter's family members that they should not have minded when Peter wrote about them.

Peter graduated *cum laude* from Kenyon College while Cal finished *summa cum laude*, Phi Beta Kappa, highest honors in classics, first man in his class and valedictorian.

Cal married Jean Stafford before graduation, and the two went to Louisiana State University in the fall of 1940 to study with Robert Penn Warren and Cleanth Brooks, both geniuses in the world of literature. Peter then sold "A Spinster's Tale" to *Southern Review* for $145 (a princely sum in those days) before following Cal and Jean to LSU. Getting a fellowship, as had Lowell, Peter rented a room from the Warrens while he was attending school. Peter said in later years that they learned not only about writing but also about how to live. Rather heavy drinking accompanied lively discussions of the writer's role many times at the dinner tables of Warren and Brooks.

By Thanksgiving, Peter Taylor had had two more stories ("The Fancy Woman" and "Winged Chariot," later named "Sky Line") published by the *Southern Review* and a poem in the *Kenyon Review*; a publisher had expressed interest in Peter's novel, and he was becoming known in literary circles. He then quit LSU because he believed he was not meant to be in a university setting and didn't have the temperament of an educator. Red Warren said that Peter asserted that he was leaving to be a writer and assured Warren that he was not in any way responsible for Peter's leaving LSU.

Peter remained in Baton Rouge until the spring to write. Warren had left to teach at the University of Iowa, so the apartment was sublet to the Lowells. Jean and Peter were very close friends by this time (with Jean being very possessive of Peter, as she was with her other male friends).

Peter Taylor returned to Memphis and was drafted in 1941. He claimed in later years that he had filled out conscientious objector forms that were then thrown away by a former girlfriend who worked at the draft office and was sure he didn't mean them. He told a friend in 1941, however, that the forms were too long to be bothered with so he sent them back not filled out. At any rate, he was sent to Fort Oglethorpe, Georgia, near Chattanooga, where he was stationed for over two years; his assignment was for clerical duty in the transportation section (thanks to intervention by the editor of the Memphis *Commercial Appeal*), the camp being run by Memphis society boys for the most part.

Peter took a room in Chattanooga, where he stayed two to five nights a week with lax supervision from Camp Oglethorpe at the time. After Pearl Harbor was bombed, of course, this ended.

In April, 1943, on one of his frequent visits to Monteagle at the home of Allan Tate and his wife, Caroline Gordon, Peter was introduced to Eleanor Ross from North Carolina; she was attending Vanderbilt on the sole writing scholarship given for 1942–43. Peter claimed later that when he saw her walking up to the door, he knew he would marry her. Eleanor was, at the time, already engaged to a doctor serving in the army. By the end of the weekend, Peter told Eleanor he was coming to Nashville the next weekend. He kept his word, and they spent hours walking and talking in Centennial Park. He extended his weekend but had to go back to Memphis for the rest of his furlough because he had promised his mother a visit. Two weeks later, he was back in Nashville, and they became engaged.

On June 4, 1943, Peter and Eleanor were married at St. Andrew's Episcopal Chapel near Sewanee. Allan Tate gave the bride away with his wife, Caroline, serving as mother of the bride. Peter's parents showed up unexpectedly with his sister Sally, some friends and champagne to celebrate the occasion. Cal Lowell was Peter's best man, and Jean Stafford was the attendant for Eleanor.

Eleanor wore a long white dress and a veil made by her friends and her. Peter had on his army uniform while Tate sported a white suit. Friends from Chattanooga and Nashville arrived and celebrated into the night as the couple left for their new apartment in Missionary Ridge near Chattanooga.

Peter and Eleanor were married for fifty-one years until Peter's death on November 2, 1994. They had two children, Katherine Baird Taylor and Peter Ross Taylor.

Peter was transferred to Camp Tidworth in England in February, 1944. After being discharged as a sergeant in December 1945, he worked at Henry Holt Publishers in New York beginning in April 1946; the couple lived in a rented apartment in Greenwich Village. In the fall of 1946, Peter accepted a position in the English Department of the Woman's College of the University of North Carolina. The next year, the Randall Jarrells and the Taylors bought a duplex in Greensboro, the first of about thirty houses that the Taylors were to own.

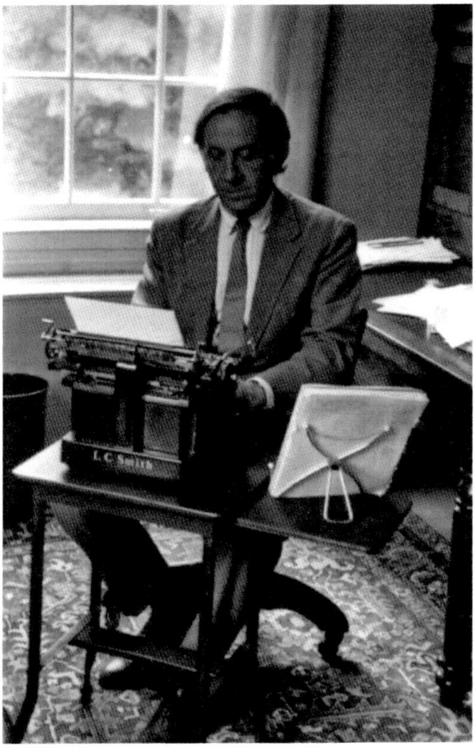

Peter Taylor. *Albert and Shirley Small Special Collections Library, University of Virginia.*

Peter Taylor used Nashville, Memphis and St. Louis in many of his stories. Trenton became "Thornton" and Monteagle—where Eleanor, the children and he were to spend many of their summers—became "Oak Mountain" in his writing. He seamlessly wove the truth of his history into his fiction so that it became a new reality.

## ACCOMPLISHMENTS

Peter Taylor's books include *A Long Fourth and Other Stories* (1948) with an introduction by Robert Penn Warren; *A Woman of Means* (1950 and reprinted in 1984); *The Widows of Thornton* (1954); *Happy Families Are All Alike* (1959); *Miss Leonora When Last Seen and Fifteen Other Stories* (1963); *The Collected Stories of Peter Taylor* (1969); *Presences: Seven Dramatic Pieces* (1973); *In the Miro District and Other Stories* (1977); *The Old Forest and Other Stories* (1985); *A Summons to Memphis* (1986); a limited edition of *A Stand in the Mountains* (a play); *The Oracle at Stoneleigh Court* (1993); and *In the Tennessee Country* (1994).

The memorial *Randall Jarrell, 1914–1965* was edited by Robert Penn Warren, Robert Lowell and Peter Taylor in 1967.

Peter's work was published in *River*, *Southern Review*, *Kenyon Review*, the *New Yorker*, *Sewanee Review*, *Shenandoah* and the *New Review*.

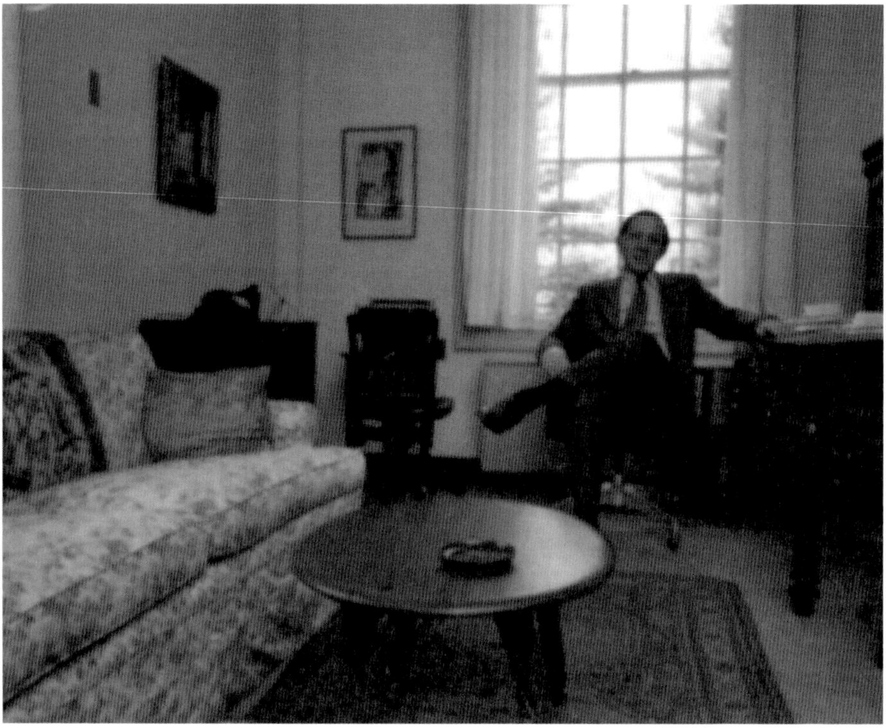

Peter Taylor. *Albert and Shirley Small Special Collections Library, University of Virginia.*

Over his lifetime, Peter Taylor won a Guggenheim Fellowship (1950–51); a National Institute of Arts and Letters Grant (1952); a Fulbright grant (1955–56); the O. Henry first prize and the Ohioana Book Award for "Venus, Cupid, Folly and Time" in 1959; a Ford Foundation Fellowship to work at the Royal Court Theater in London in 1960; a Rockefeller Foundation grant for a school year of writing only (1966–67); the Gold Medal for the Short Story from the American Academy and Institute in 1978; a $25,000 senior fellowship from the National Endowment for the Arts in recognition of his extraordinary contribution to American literature in 1984; the PEN/Faulkner Award for Fiction for *The Old Forest and Other Stories* (1986); the Ritz Hemingway Prize and the Pulitzer Prize for Fiction in 1987; and Italy's *Chianti Ruffino Antico Fattore* International Literary in 1989. He was inducted into the National Institute of Arts and Letters on May 21, 1969 and the American Academy of Arts and Letters in May 1978.

Peter Taylor taught at Indiana University, Woman's College (twice), the University of North Carolina (as professor of English), the University

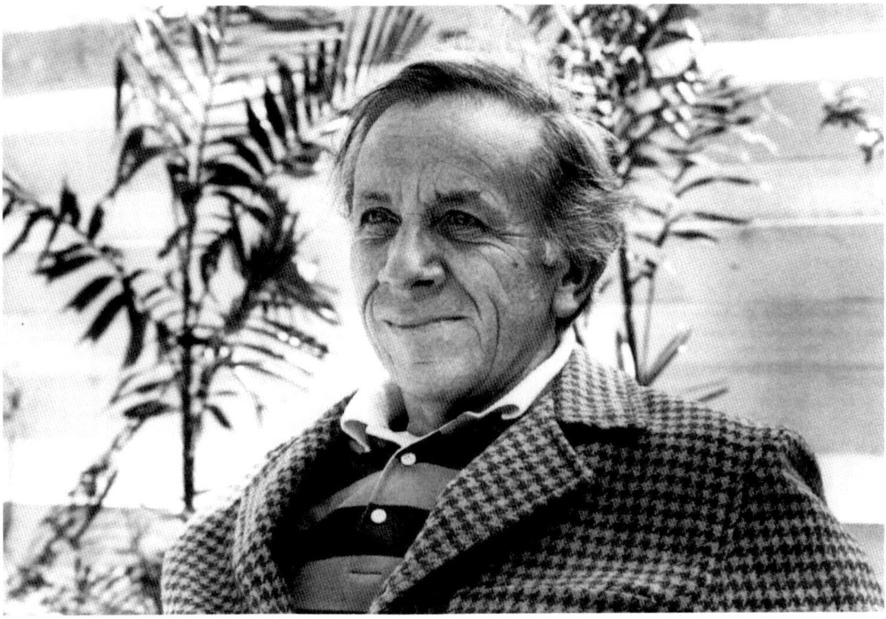

Peter Taylor. *Albert and Shirley Small Special Collections Library, University of Virginia.*

of Chicago, Kenyon College, Ohio State University, Harvard University, Oxford University, the University of Georgia, Memphis State University and retired from the University of Virginia in 1983.

## ELEANOR ROSS TAYLOR

*Eleanor has simply made it all possible.*
*Peter Taylor*

No discussion of the life of Peter Taylor would be complete without the spotlight searching out his beloved wife, Eleanor. Her own career as a poet gleaned national awards, but her path was delayed to some extent by her devotion not only to her husband but also to their two children.

Eleanor was born on June 30, 1920, in Norwood, North Carolina. Her parents were Fred Elbert Ross and Jennie Catherine Lilly Ross. She had two brothers, James and Fred, and one sister, Jean, all of whom became writers. Eleanor earned her undergraduate degree at Woman's College at the

University of North Carolina. She ended her graduate study at Vanderbilt when she married Peter Taylor. A teetotaler and a person who never learned to drive, she was a wife and mother first. She loved to garden and to read. With Peter, she enjoyed renovating old houses and buying additional ones for renovation.

Peter Taylor once revealed that after their children were grown, Eleanor and he loved to work in their pajamas until lunchtime at two in the afternoon. They worked on opposite ends of the house, usually with Eleanor in the upper story and Peter in the basement, so that they could not hear the typewriter of the other. (It seems that when one was typing and the other was not, it caused stress for the one who was "blocked" at the time.)

Poet Eleanor Ross Taylor published *Wilderness of Ladies* in 1960 followed by five other collections of her poetry—*Welcome Eumenides* (1972), *New and Selected Poems* (1983), *Days Going/Days Coming Back* (1991), *Late Leisure* (1999) and *Captive Voices: New and Selected Poems* (2009).

Special Collections at the Jean and Alexander Heard Library of Vanderbilt University has a number of family letters to and from Eleanor; it also contains a few letters from Peter to Eleanor from the days he was stationed in England during World War II. The letters reveal Eleanor's genteel and affectionate nature, as she wrote often to Peter's mother. They speak of the everyday life experiences during World War II as she attempts to send Peter socks, razor blades and other items he needs. It is evident also that Peter's mother sent packages often to Eleanor and Peter throughout her life, as Eleanor thanks her for her generosity.

Eleanor changed jobs several times while Peter was away at war. She worked not only in libraries but also as a teacher in various schools.

A few letters in the collection are from 1979, when Peter and Eleanor lived at 1841 Wayside Place in Charlottesville, Virginia. Eleanor mentions their neighbor, Edward "Eddy" von Selzam, a former German diplomat who retired from his career in insurance and lived across the street from the Taylors. He was well known in Charlottesville for his "Sunday afternoons," drop-in cocktail parties at which the elite of society from not only the University of Virginia but also the Farmington Country Club set were seen. Peter was an occasional visitor in Eddy's home, but it was not the kind of event that Eleanor craved.

Before her death at age ninety-one on December 30, 2011 in Falls Church, Virginia, Eleanor won the Poetry Society of America's Shelley Memorial Prize (1997–98), a fellowship with the American Academy of Arts and Letters (1998), the Library of Virginia's Literary Award for Poetry (2000), the Aiken Taylor Award for Modern Poetry (2001), the Carole Weinstein Poetry Prize (2009) and the Poetry Foundation's Ruth Lilly Poetry Prize for lifetime achievements in 2010.

CHAPTER THREE

# CORMAC MCCARTHY

## *FROM KNOXVILLE TO SECLUSION*

*I just think I've been very lucky...I'm one of the luckiest people I've ever known...I've done nothing to be picked out.*
Cormac McCarthy

The life of Cormac McCarthy is no secret. It is widely known that he was born in Providence, Rhode Island, on July 20, 1933. He was the third of six children in a Roman Catholic family. His parents were Charles Joseph and Gladys Christina McGrail McCarthy. He had two brothers and three sisters.

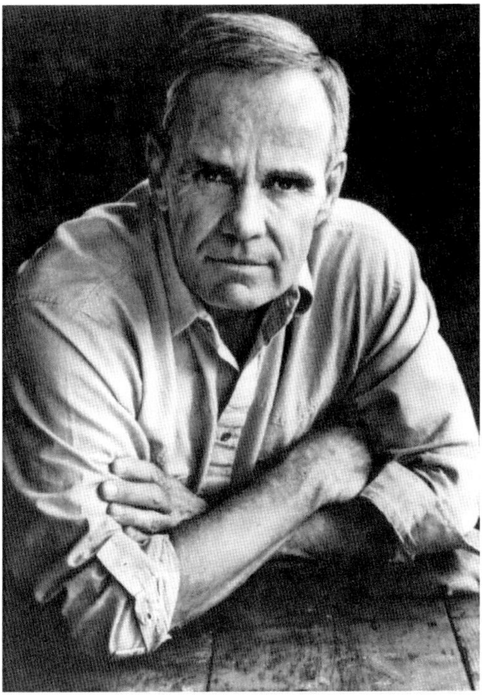

Cormac McCarthy. *University Historian Collection, AR 0015, Box 83, University of Tennessee Libraries, Knoxville, Special Collections.*

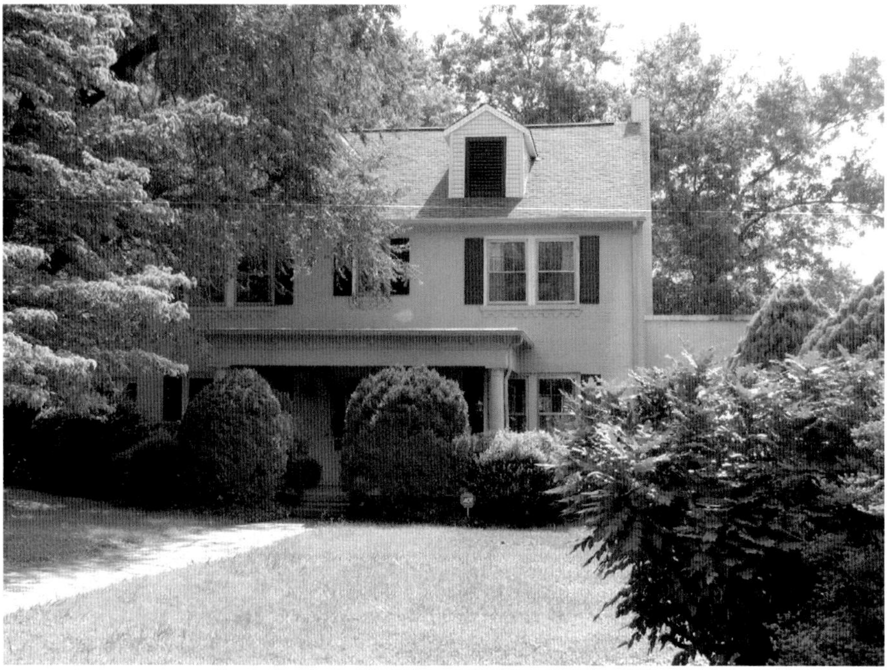

Cormac McCarthy's childhood home in Knoxville. *Courtesy of J.M. White.*

## CHILDHOOD AND EDUCATION

*I like what I do.*
*Cormac McCarthy*

Originally named Charles, he renamed himself Cormac after the Irish King. Some sources claim that his family had his name changed legally to the Gaelic word meaning "son of Charles."

Cormac's father, Charles Joseph McCarthy, was a lawyer for the Tennessee Valley Authority; originally on the legal staff from 1934 to 1967, he was promoted to chief counsel in 1958.

In 1937, the family moved to Knoxville, Tennessee, because of the father's job. Cormac was four at the time. Later attending Catholic High School, Cormac went on to the University of Tennessee in 1951, majoring in liberal arts. He joined the United States Air Force in 1953 and was sent to Alaska for two of the four years he served. While in Alaska, he was the host of a radio show.

After leaving the air force, he returned to UT and published in the literary magazine, the *Phoenix*, two stories—"A Drowning Incident" and "Wake for

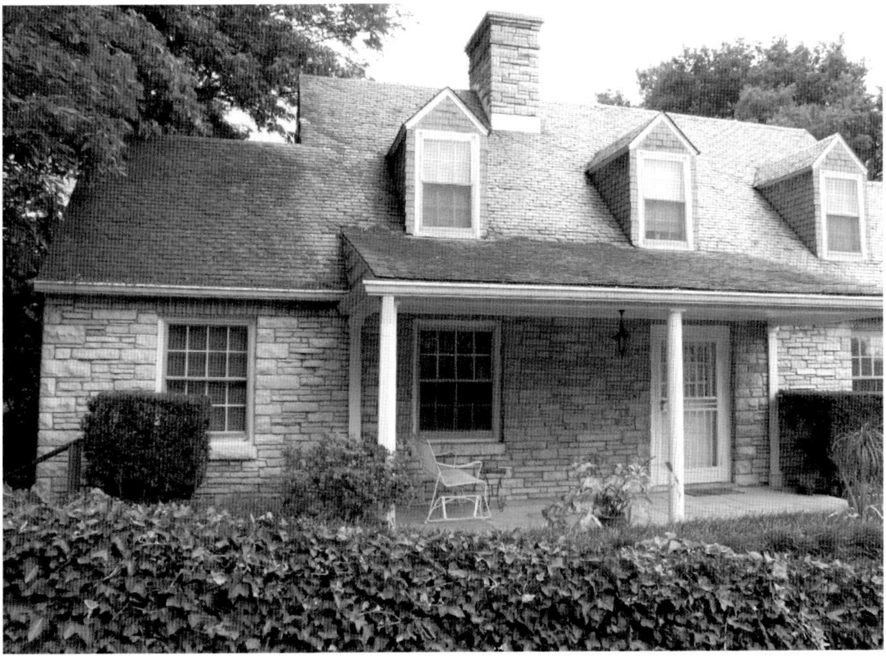

Home in Knoxville where Cormac McCarthy lived. *Courtesy of J.M. White.*

Susan." His byline was C.J. McCarthy Jr. In both 1959 and 1960, he won the Ingram-Merrill Award for creative writing; he was still a student at the time.

Believing that his role in life would be that of a writer, he left UT and moved to Chicago, where he took a job as an automobile mechanic. During that time, he wrote his first novel, *The Orchard Keeper*, winner of the Faulkner Award. He married Lee Holleman, also a former student from the University of Tennessee. (The Cormac McCarthy Society describes the marriage as occurring in Chicago, but some writers claim that they were married while in school in Knoxville.)

## FIRST MARRIAGE

*Women are tough...I don't pretend to understand women.*
*Cormac McCarthy*

According to her obituary in the *Bakersfield Californian*, Lee Holleman was a native of Arkansas before attending the University of Tennessee. This version states that she married Cormac McCarthy during their college years, and they moved into an unheated shack with no running water outside Knoxville. (The obituary doesn't mention their living in Chicago. Most versions of this story have the couple moving to Sevier County, Tennessee, after having lived in Chicago.) All versions agree that they had one son, Cullen, who was born in 1962. The marriage lasted four years.

The *Bakersfield Californian* relates that while Lee was taking care of the small child and doing housework, she was asked by Cormac to get a job so that he could write. At that point, she left him and moved to Wyoming, where she filed for divorce. She taught school there for two years and then moved to Bakersfield and taught in Kern County. Earning a master's degree at San Francisco State University, she moved back to Kern County and taught at Wasco Union High School, where she received the Arts Council of Kern's Individual Arts Educator Award. In 1975, she received a Stegner Fellowship to Stanford University. In 1991, she was the corecipient of the Nicholas Roerich Prize in poetry for her collection *Desire's Door*. Her chapbook *Combing Hair with a Seashell* won the Ion Books National Chapbook Competition in 1992. She also published another

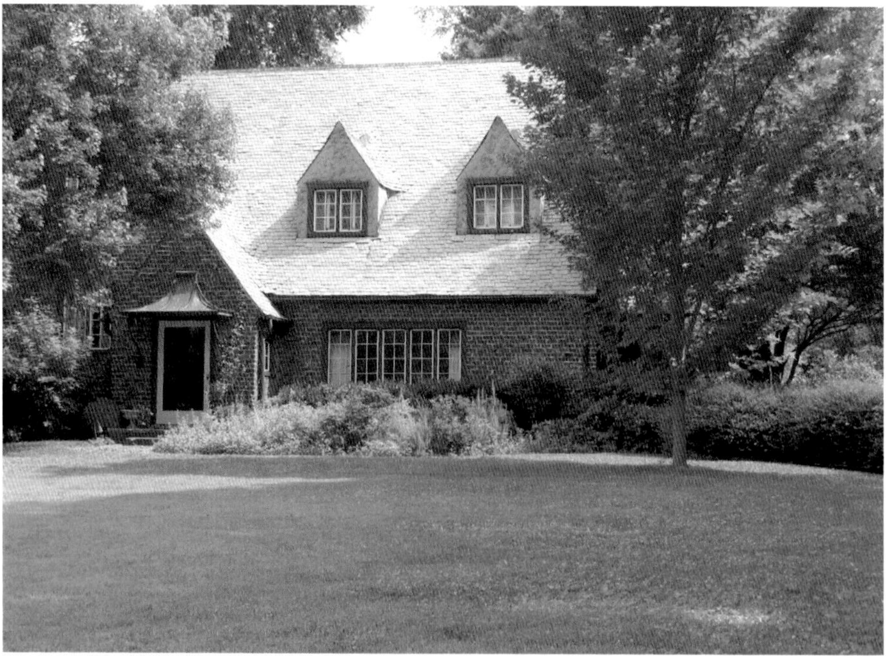

Another of Cormac McCarthy's houses in Knoxville. *Courtesy of J.M. White.*

book of poetry, *Good Girl*, and wrote for *Orpheus*, *Great River Review*, *Solo*, *Third Coast*, *Daybreak*, *Pangolin*, *High Plains Literary Review*, *Raccoon*, *Arizona Literary Magazine*, *Burnt Sienna* and *Into 8*.

Lee Holleman McCarthy died on March 21, 2009, at the age of seventy.

## EARLY BOOKS

*You can't plot everything out. You just have to trust where it comes from.*
*Cormac McCarthy*

Cormac McCarthy's first editor was Albert Erskine, who was also William Faulkner's editor, at Random House. He claimed he sent his work there because it was the only publishing house he'd ever heard of.

Prior to the publication of *The Orchard Keeper* in 1965, McCarthy had received that same year a traveling fellowship from the American Academy of Arts and Letters. He left the United States on the liner *Sylvania* with a plan to visit the home of his Irish ancestors; King Cormac MacCarthy is reputed to have given to Ireland the "Blarney Stone" that people kiss at Blarney Castle.

On the ship, Cormac met Anne DeLisle, an English singer and dancer, whom he married in England in 1966. He received a Rockefeller Grant for 1966 to 1968, so they toured England, France, Switzerland, Italy and Spain during that time. Discovering a type of artist's colony on the island of Ibiza, they settled there for McCarthy to complete the revisions of *Outer Dark*. In 1967, they returned to the United States to live in Rockford, Tennessee, near Knoxville. Their domicile, according to Mrs. McCarthy, was a pig farm that they rented for fifty dollars a month. When *Outer Dark* was published in 1968, it, like *The Orchard Keeper*, received good reviews.

*I was always naïve. I always believed I would be taken care of.*
*Cormac McCarthy*

The Guggenheim Fellowship for creative writing was awarded to Cormac in 1969. The couple then moved into a barn near Louisville, Tennessee, where McCarthy renovated the barn entirely on his own—even cutting and kiln drying the wood and building the chimney and a stone room. The new fireplace was made from bricks that Cormac salvaged from the boyhood home of James Agee when it was leveled for urban renewal in Knoxville.

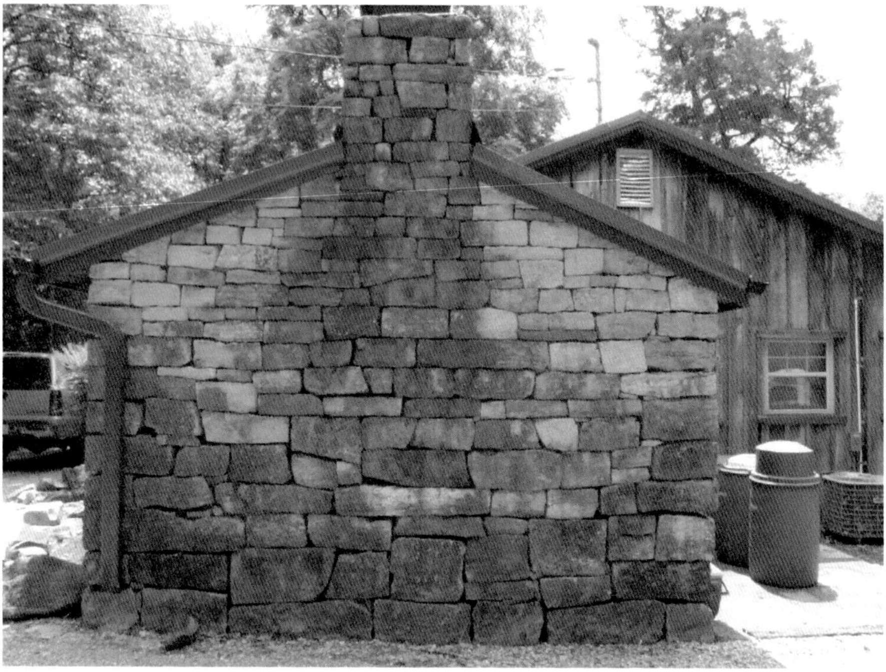

House where Cormac McCarthy used stones from James Agee's former house. *Courtesy of J.M. White.*

> *I opened up the letter and in it was a check for $20,000. I was the first recipient of a fellowship.*
>
> *Cormac McCarthy*

In 1973, Cormac McCarthy completed *Child of God*, which was published later that year. The novel, to no one's surprise, received mixed reviews. The leading character, Lester Ballard, loses his land and proceeds to become a "Peeping Tom" and, later, a necrophiliac. It is a book that critics either love or hate.

From 1974 through 1975, McCarthy wrote a screenplay, *The Gardener's Son*, for a PBS film; it premiered in January, 1977 and was based on real events in South Carolina. It was revised and later published by Ecco Press. The film won two Emmy Award nominations and was shown at the Berlin and Edinburgh Film Festivals. The plot involves the murder of a mill owner by a former employee who is angry at the treatment of the millworkers; the theme is class differences in America. It is Southern Gothic to put it mildly.

Having had no children, Cormac McCarthy and Anne DeLisle separated in 1976. Richard B. Woodward, in his April 1992 *New York Times* review, "Cormac McCarthy's Venomous Fiction," quotes Anne DeLisle as describing their life together while living in the dairy barn as eating beans and bathing in the lake in spite of offers for Cormac to speak for a couple thousand dollars at some university or other; he'd turn the offer down and tell them that he'd already said everything in the books. Their marriage lasted (amazingly) eight years.

> *I always knew that I didn't want to work.*
>
> *Cormac McCarthy*

The secret of McCarthy's success with other human beings seems to be that he is eminently charming, although, at the time of Woodward's article, McCarthy was cutting his own hair, washing his clothes at a laundromat, eating either in a cafeteria or off a hot plate and living in a tiny stone cottage in El Paso. He claimed to own seven thousand books, most of which were in storage. On the other hand, he had many friends, all of whom knew he liked to be left alone, but McCarthy was described as a great conversationalist who had a terrific sense of humor and who liked to laugh.

## MATURE NOVELS

By 1979, *Suttree*, whom many claim is his best novel, was published—but again, it received both positive and negative reviews. Shelby Foote, the well-known novelist and historian, actually rebuked a reviewer (in a letter to the editor) in the *Memphis Press Scimitar* for his negative review of *Suttree*.

By 1981, McCarthy was living in a motel room in Knoxville when he learned that he was the recipient of the MacArthur Foundation Fellowship, the commonly known "genius" grant. He used the money to live on while he wrote *Blood Meridian*, published in 1985. Researching this book heavily and basing it on historical events in Texas and Mexico around 1840, Cormac learned Spanish as he visited the places he wrote about in the book. Although it received scant attention at the time it was published, *Blood Meridian* is now considered second only to *Suttree* as his finest writing. It was named one of *Time* magazine's top one hundred books written in English from 1923 to 2005.

When Albert Erskine retired from Random House, McCarthy moved to Alfred A. Knopf, where Gary Fisketjon was assigned to be his editor. At that point, McCarthy gained more exposure for his work. He granted his only interview to the *New York Times Magazine*. In 1992, *All the Pretty Horses* was published as the first volume of the Border Trilogy. A publishing sensation with excellent reviews, it sold 190,000 copies during the first six months and entered the *New York Times* Bestseller List. The money from the book paid for a new pickup truck for McCarthy, who kept on writing. *All the Pretty Horses* won the National Book Award for Fiction and the National Book Critics' Circle Award, both in 1992.

The movie *All the Pretty Horses* came out in 2000 with Matt Damon as John Grady Cole, Penelope Cruz as Alejandra and Henry Thomas as Lacey Rawlins. Billy Bob Thornton was the director. It was nominated for the Paris Film Festival Grand Prix in 2001 and was nominated for a number of other awards including the Golden Boot Award (Best of the West).

> *The unconscious is always with you…Someone in my head is making up what I'm going to do next.*
>
> *Cormac McCarthy*

*The Stonemason*, a novel about the lives of three generations of a black family in Kentucky, was published in 1994 by Ecco Press. It was closely followed by *The Crossing*, the second volume of the Border Trilogy. It had a 200,000 first print run (highly unusual for literary fiction) but soon was followed by a second printing of 25,000. Billy Parham is the protagonist, and the reader follows his attempt to take a she-wolf back home to Mexico.

About the time that *Cities of the Plain*, the last volume of the Border Trilogy, was published in 1998, Cormac McCarthy married Jennifer Winkley. Their son, John Francis, was born in 1999. They moved from El Paso to Tesque, New Mexico, near Santa Fe, where McCarthy is now writer-in-residence for the Santa Fe Institute.

> *Usually you don't know where a book comes from.*
>
> *Cormac McCarthy*

*No Country for Old Men* was published in 2005 and was promptly made into a movie (2007) by Joel and Ethan Coen. The movie starred Tommy Lee Jones as Ed Tom Bell, Javier Bardem as Anton Chigurh and Josh Brolin as Llewelyn Moss. Moss discovers $2 million that drug runners have fought and died over, takes it for himself and becomes the quarry of Chigurh, a psychopathic killer who slaughters everyone in his path. Sheriff Bell conducts the investigation of the brutal murders Chigurh commits as Moss tries to keep ahead of the killer. The movie was nominated for eight Academy Awards and won four, including Best Picture. It also won two Golden Globe Awards after being nominated for four. Additionally, it won numerous other awards including three British Academy Film Awards (BAFTA) and top honors at the Directors' Guild of America Awards for Ethan and Joel Coen.

## PULITZER PRIZE

*It came because my son almost cowrote this book.*
*Cormac McCarthy*

The publishing of *The Road* in 2006 by Alfred A. Knopf gleaned the James Tait Black Memorial Prize for Fiction in 2006 and the 2007 Pulitzer Prize for Literature for Cormac McCarthy, who has said that his son was the inspiration for the book. With international acclaim, *The Road* was made into a movie in 2009 starring Viggo Mortensen as the Man, Kodi Smit-McPhee as the Boy and Charlize Theron as the Woman.

Oprah Winfrey named *The Road* for the April 2007 Book of the Month; consequently, Cormac agreed to his first and only television interview, which took place at the Santa Fe Institute Library and aired on June 5, 2007. He stated in the interview that he didn't know any writers but preferred the company of scientists. (Most quotations in this section are from that interview.)

Interestingly, at some time when McCarthy lived in Knoxville, he received a phone call from a writer who was unknown at the time. The man's name was William Gay; they discussed books and became friends over the telephone. Eventually, McCarthy realized that William was a writer and asked him to send him some of his work. He influenced the writing of William Gay and even edited part of one of his early manuscripts, *Provinces of Night*.

*The Sunset Limited*, a play, was also published by McCarthy in 2006. It was performed on HBO in 2011 with Samuel L. Jackson playing Black and Tommy Lee Jones as White. Black rescues White from a suicide attempt after which they discuss the absurdity of the human condition and the existence of God.

In 2012, an announcement was made that McCarthy had written a screenplay called *The Counselor*, but little is known about it except that Ridley Scott is to be the director.

## INTERESTING FACTS

*Punctuation is to make it easier, not to make it harder.*
*Cormac McCarthy*

The Olivetti typewriter that McCarthy had used for forty-six years was auctioned at Christie's in 2009, according to *Wired* magazine. The original purchase price was $50, and it was bought in a Knoxville pawnshop. It brought $254,500 (after Christie's had estimated it would bring between $15,000 and $20,000). John Miller, a friend, gave McCarthy another Olivetti that cost $11. Not surprisingly, the proceeds of the auction went to Santa Fe Institute for scientific research.

Cormac McCarthy has his own rules for writing—no semicolons, no quotation marks for dialogue and preferred use of simple declarative sentences. He does not wish to be annoyed by the public and spends most of his time at the Santa Fe Institute. He can be reached (if ever) only through his agent. Having endured periods in his life of both feast and famine, he chooses to be left alone.

CHAPTER FOUR

# WILLIAM GAY

## *THE MAN FROM HOHENWALD*

*As a kid I lived in a house in the middle of the woods. The trees came right up to the door. We had no air conditioning, no electricity.*
*William Gay*

He lived out the end of his life in a log house next to Little Swan Creek in Hohenwald, Tennessee; sometimes, he wrote in the treehouse in his front yard. He didn't seek fame or fortune; he just wanted to be a writer. His first short stories were published when he was fifty-seven years old after he discovered the literary magazines that many colleges produce. One of his novels was at the top of the best books list that Stephen King chose in 2007.

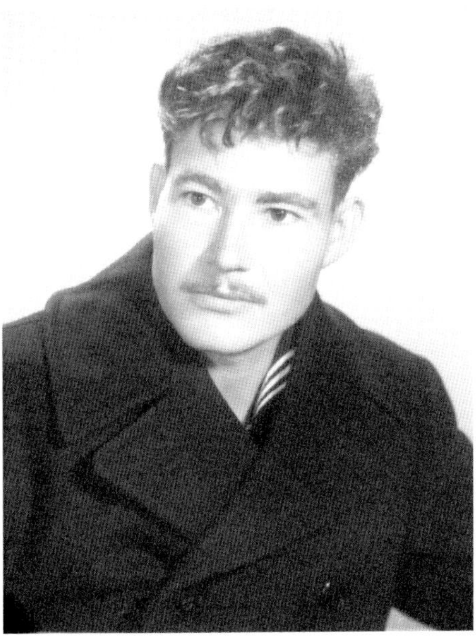
William Gay, about 1960. *Courtesy of William Gay Jr.; photo of original by J.M. White.*

His name was William Elbert Gay; he was born on October 27, 1941. (For years, this date was published over and over as being in 1943, but that was a mistake. His brother insists that William was born in 1939. No birth certificate has been located, so the jury is out.)

## Childhood

Growing up in Grinders Creek, Tennessee, near a deserted mining town that later became "Harrikin" in his books, William was not the child you would have picked to become a world-class author. His parents were poor because his father, Arthur, was a sharecropper and sometimes worked in a sawmill. Nobody in his family was a reader, yet William devoured books all his life. He seemed not to need the amount of sleep that other people required and usually read most or all of the night (if he wasn't writing).

A favorite of the school librarian, he had once asked her how much she had to pay to be able to work with all those books. Once she learned that he was interested in drawing, she would let him borrow coffee-table art books that were never supposed to leave the library.

When his seventh-grade teacher found out he was reading Zane Grey westerns, he offered William a copy of *Look Homeward, Angel* by Thomas Wolfe. William loved the book but remembered years later that because there was no electricity in their house, his mother demanded that he blow out the kerosene lamp to save money. He had to wait until daylight to keep reading. After reading a couple of books by Wolfe, William decided that if you could read, you could write too. He always claimed he got high off writing the way a heroin junkie might off drugs.

> *I always thought that being a writer was the highest thing that you could aspire to do.*
>
> *William Gay*

When he was a boy, William was able to buy Signet books in the drugstore for thirty-five cents. Acquiring a lifelong fascination with Southern gothic literature, he read every book by Truman Capote he could get his hands on, but the best thirty-five cents he ever spent, he insisted, was *A Good Man Is Hard to Find* by Flannery O'Connor.

By the time he was in eighth grade, he was writing his first novel, a western called *East of the Moon, West of the Sun*. Even then, he was using his own brand of punctuation. He believed that writers should be allowed no exclamation points, three semi-colons, no quotation marks and very few commas for a lifetime.

He received at some time early in his life a rejection slip advising him that the publishing house did not accept handwritten manuscripts.

(William's older son, Chris, believes that his father threw away about fifteen or sixteen books that he wrote when he was young because he didn't think they were any good.)

One of William's boyhood jobs was working in a furniture store in Hohenwald (German for "high forest"). A man who would come in to tell William stories about various happenings in the area once mentioned that there were abandoned wells in the area where some people who had disappeared had ended up. That information stuck in William's head for years and later appeared on the pages of *The Long Home*, his first published novel.

> *During the writing, you just have to believe another scene will present itself when you're done with the one in hand. You've got to keep that faith.*
>
> *William Gay*

## The Early Years

After he finished high school, he joined the navy but continued to write. His subject matter, he admitted, was exotic people in exotic places, about which he knew little or nothing. He said until he finally started writing about his own roots, he hadn't found his voice.

Because he believed you needed to live in New York or Chicago to be a writer, he moved to both locations after he completed four years in the navy. It is said that he worked in a cardboard-box factory in New York and a pinball-machine factory in Chicago. Like everybody, he had to eat.

A lover of all Bob Dylan songs, he played one song, "Don't Think Twice; It's All Right," so much that his girlfriend left him over it. He didn't seem to think it was a great loss. His musical knowledge was encyclopedic; in later life, he wrote a music column for the *Oxford American*, and his close friends all talk about the hours they would spend talking music with William.

Discovering *The Orchard Keeper* by Cormac McCarthy showed William Gay that he too could write about his own area of the country. William was a dedicated fan of Cormac. "That name was like that of a god in our house when I was growing up," his son Chris insists. William himself told

Georgia Afton in an interview that Cormac McCarthy "is an alchemist with words. He's the best writer working, and he's better than a bunch of dead ones, too."

After he learned from McCarthy that "landscape has to be tactile; you have to smell it, feel it, inhabit it," William let setting become an important part of everything he wrote because he came to believe that books without "deference to place and time and weather never seem real to me." He talked about the fact that he liked to write about snow and claimed that his talisman was nature. "It carries a sort of magic that I can take out and draw on to ground myself and my characters."

> *I'm a serious writer because I believe in what I do. I never wrote with a paycheck in mind.*
>
> *William Gay*

Throughout his life, William worked hard at things other than writing because it took many years before he began to publish. Some of the jobs he had were working at a drive-in, a television-tube assembly line and all types of construction work, including laying bricks and working as a painter, a carpenter and a dry-wall hanger.

## PERSONAL INTIMATIONS

The first time I heard William read at the Clarksville Writers' Conference, he was reading from a book that his good friend Sonny Brewer had put together called *Don't Quit Your Day Job: Acclaimed Authors and the Day Jobs They Quit*. William, who had a never-ending sense of wry humor, remarked that when Sonny asked him to write a chapter in this book about the sorriest job he'd ever had, he had a hard time choosing because there was some stiff competition for the title. He chose to write about working in a boat-paddle factory, and the results were hilarious.

A famous quotation from *Provinces of Night* is when Fleming's grandmother tells him, "If sense was gunpowder ever' one of you men put together wouldn't have enough to load a round of birdshot."

William seems to have chosen work that didn't require mental concentration—he was writing in his mind while his hands were moving—and he didn't talk to the other guys at work about his writing either. Most of

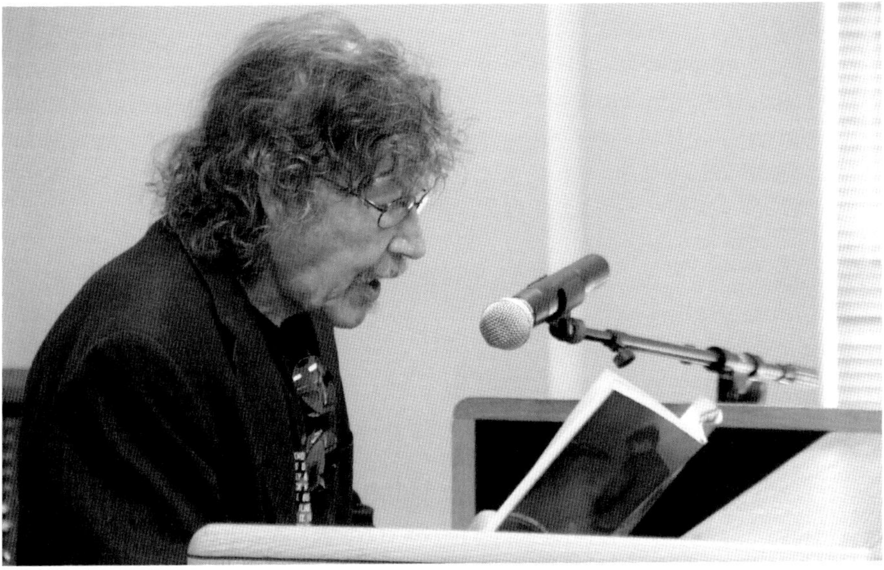

William Gay reading at Clarksville Writers' Conference. *Bill Larson.*

the people he worked with were much more interested in hunting or fishing than "the sonnet you wrote over the weekend."

> *To my kids I was a Pa Ingalls from* Little House on the Prairie, *just a straight, hardworking guy who never lost his temper…I wanted to be a great father and have my kids love me, which worked, I guess, because we're very close.*
>
> *William Gay*

## FAMILY LIFE

William said he married early and became the father of four children; Lee, born on October 16, 1969; Christopher David, born on July 18, 1974; Laura, born on September 20, 1975; and William Blake, born on July 1, 1981. William always had a special tone in his voice when he talked of his children. You could feel the love coming through him. (His marriage to Dianne Bowen ended in divorce after all the children were grown.)

"We always had a special time at Christmas," Chris remembered, one of his most vivid memories of his childhood. "We'd all go out in the woods and cut down the tree together."

William was deeply engaged in the lives of his children. After working hard physically all day, he'd read every night to the kids before bedtime. "We never needed a dictionary or encyclopedia when we were growing up. If we needed to know something, we'd just go ask Dad," Chris related at a memorial tribute to his father. "I thought all fathers were like that."

In his later years, when his daughter Laura was diagnosed with cancer, William didn't leave home for long. Even though he was offered the Renée and John Grisham Chair of Creative Writing at the University of Mississippi, he turned it down to be close to Laura. His precious Cormac McCarthy letters were sold to provide for her care, along with paintings and manuscripts. William put his children first above everything else in his life.

While his children were young, William would write after they went to sleep. As he had been since preadolescence, he was sending out manuscripts to the *Atlantic*, the *New Yorker*, *Harper's*, *Esquire* and other magazines constantly. It was not until he learned about the collegiate literary magazines that he became a published author.

> *I just always thought I knew what I was doing even if the editors obviously thought otherwise.*
>
> *William Gay*

## PUBLICATION

In 1973, Cormac McCarthy's *Child of God* came out. After William read it, he had some questions. In a totally uncharacteristic move, he called Information in Knoxville and was given McCarthy's phone number. When the phone rang, McCarthy actually answered. He wasn't thrilled to hear William asking about his own books, but when the magic words "Flannery O'Conner" came up, a connection was made. Although William claimed not to have a photographic memory, he could remember long passages from many books he loved. The two men then swapped their favorite paragraphs and decided to speak together again.

Cormac McCarthy was a great influence on the writing of William Gay. After they had spoken a few times on the phone, McCarthy asked William if he were a writer and, learning that he was, told William to send him some of his work. He gave William assistance with certain aspects of his prose. William said that he had a tendency at first to use the same word too many times—after the fourth "moon" on one page, McCarthy had written "too many moons."

They exchanged a few letters, and McCarthy actually mailed William an unpublished manuscript at one point, which William sent it back to him. The manuscript was for *Suttree*, according to William, and this was confirmed by William's brother.

> *I think the most important thing is to write a scene so whoever's reading it recognizes it. They* [might] *not recognize the actual situation, but the emotion, whatever emotion the scene evokes.*
>
> *William Gay*

William Gay truly believed that the publishing of McCarthy's *All the Pretty Horses* in 1992 and Charles Frazier's *Cold Mountain* in 2003 gave East Coast editors a "heads up" on Southern writers and their place in the forefront of writing once more. He attributed this to the fact that his writing was eventually published.

Marc Smirnoff at *Oxford American* bemoans the fact that he rejected William's stories after John Jeremiah Sullivan, then associate editor at *OA*, kept pressing them on him. He said that *OA* could have been the first to publish William Gay but the *Missouri Review* had that honor in 1998 when "Those Deep Elm Brown's Ferry Blues" graced its pages. The *Georgia Review* then published "I Hate to See That Evening Sun Go Down," and William Gay's life began to change.

What Marc Smirnoff did, however, was referred to by William years later when he was speaking on a literary panel. He said that the long letters of rejection had helped sustain him because they showed that Smirnoff had faith in his work—and William said he liked the letters and had kept them. (In the meantime, Smirnoff was in fear and trembling that the audience, who was in the palm of William's hand by this time, might turn on Smirnoff and roast him on a spit.)

At the *Georgia Review*, during the time William's first short story was published, the man who bought his story was also working as an acquisitions editor for MacMurry & Beck, a small publishing company. He called William up and asked if he had a novel. Did he ever.

*The Long Home* was published in 1999. Here was the story of the old well that held a body from his childhood memory. The title, *The Long Home*, is from Ecclesiastes 12:5: "Also when they shall be afraid of that which is high, and fears shall be in the way, and the almond tree shall flourish, and the

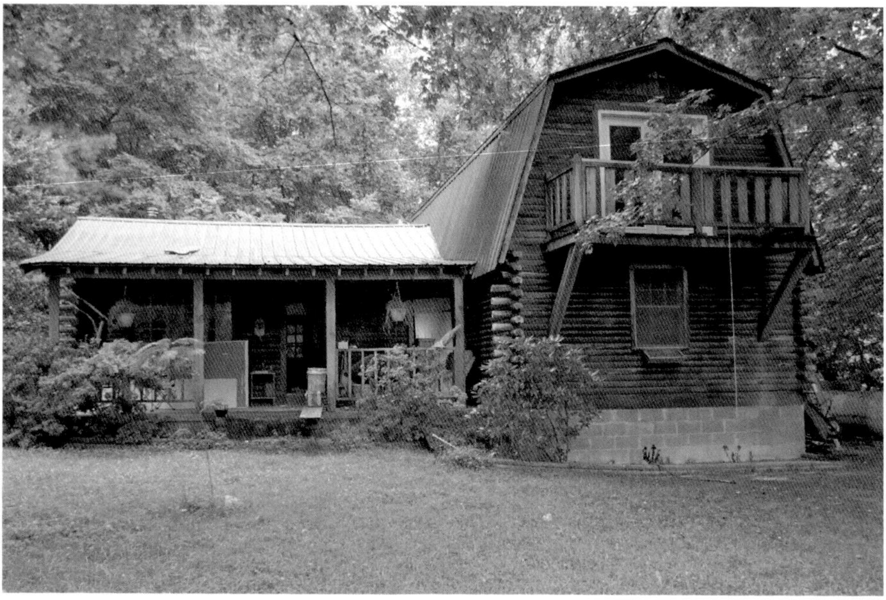

Front view of William Gay's house in Howenwald. *Bill Larson.*

grasshopper shall be a burden, and desire shall fail: because man goes to his long home, and the mourners go about the streets." (This quote graces William Gay's tombstone. According to his wishes, William was cremated; however, the family put up a stone in the cemetery on Grinder's Creek next to his parents.)

By this time, Amy Williams, an agent from New York, was tracking William down in Hohenwald. She was amused to find out that he lived on William Gay Road; when he moved away from his trailer to his log house, he actually tore down the William Gay Road street sign and mailed it to her.

When Ms. Williams first talked to William, she learned that he didn't think many people would want to read his books, but she told him that was her department. He had to admit later that she was right.

Joel Tomlin, owner of Landmark Booksellers in Franklin, Tennessee, and a close friend of William, said that the first time he ever saw William Gay, he was going to sign books in the David-Kidd Bookstore (now out of business, but for many years a mecca for book lovers in Nashville). Joel said that every foot of the building where someone could stand was filled to capacity. When William entered the room, you could see on his face the absolute awe that all those people had come to see him.

Sonny Brewer, another close friend of William, drove him to Maine to a book signing where, they were told, more people had come to see William than even for Robert Frost or John Irving.

> *Whatever impulse is driving you to tell the story has to be surrendered to. You have to give it its head…Let it take wing on its own.*
>
> *William Gay*

William said that he was going through his divorce when he was writing *Provinces of Night* (published in 2000), so he was living alone for the first time in a long time. He had more time to write, so it took him only four or five months to complete the book.

*Provinces of Night* was made into a movie, *Bloodworth*, starring Kris Kristofferson, Val Kilmer and Hilary Duff. William never went to see it because the screenwriters changed a number of things from the book. He understood that it was too expensive to recreate the 1950s, so the director, Shane Dax Taylor, moved the setting to contemporary times. The drunks and bootleggers became drug dealers.

Kris Kristofferson called William up to tell him he was sorry that he was unable to come to the movie set and that he would have liked to hang out with him. (William's daughter was quite ill at the time, and he wouldn't leave her.) All of William's children eventually saw the movie, however.

> *The reader instinctively knows if there's a hand on the wheel, if somebody's in control who knows what he's talking about. One whiff of disbelief and your book's a paperweight.*
>
> *William Gay*

In 2002, the collection of stories *I Hate to See That Evening Sun Go Down* was published. One of the stories in this book, "The Paperhanger," has been described as one of the most bone-chilling stories ever written. William said he was once dating a woman, who after reading this story, never looked at him the same way again. He insisted that it was just a story, but nevertheless, he said, "That story warped the way she saw me. It cost me a fairly decent girlfriend." (Having been part of at least ten anthologies as of this writing, "The Paperhanger" is one of the most anthologized short stories in modern literature.)

Tom Franklin is the author of *Poachers; Hell at the Breech*; *Smonk*: *Crooked Letter, Crooked Letter*; and *The Alumni Grill: Anthology of Southern Writers*, volume two (edited with his wife, Beth Ann Fennelly). He was also the Renée and John Grisham Chair at University of Mississippi and a close friend and drinking buddy of William. He said that William wrote "The Paperhanger" after he heard the story of a plumber friend who was bitten on the ankle by a rich woman's lapdog while he was working. He whacked it with a pipe wrench and killed it. Hastily hiding the dog in his toolbox, he finished working under the sink, drove away and tossed the dead dog out the window of his vehicle.

William told Georgia Afton that, years later, he was painting a house for a Pakistani couple who had a little girl. They seemed to have an "imperial air," which later blended into his memory of the plumber's escapade. Thus the story was born.

"That Evening Sun" was made into a movie starring Hal Holbrook, whom William had met previously and liked. Dixie Carter had a cameo appearance in the movie also. It was filmed on a farm near Knoxville. Clarksvillian Shelia Kennedy, sister to the daughter-in-law of the farm owners, met William on the set. She was to become one of his closest friends in the years ahead and was his driver on more than one occasion.

Speaking of women and William Gay, Tom Franklin wrote in William's obituary in *Oxford American*, "Women loved him. They wanted to take care of him, to fatten him up."

Joel Tomlin reported that during and after one of William's readings at Joel's bookstore, Landmark Booksellers, the young women (half William's age) were "all over him."

When he was told at a writers' conference that several of the women there were interested in him, he asked, "Do they have a dog?"

Yes, William loved dogs, too. (He had a big gentle pit bull that was his constant companion at the end of his life.)

William had some idiosyncrasies, like most people. He didn't eat a lot, and he seemed to need little sleep; he'd much rather read or write. He was so widely read that you could hardly name a book he hadn't read at least once. He never went to college but was thoroughly educated on many subjects purely from reading and listening to music. He cut his own naturally curly hair, and he took baths in the creek beside his house in warm weather. When he was a boy and didn't have money for ink, he'd make it out of walnut juice. He sometimes hunted ginseng in the woods and that habit wafted its way into his writing.

When he was older, he stopped driving altogether. His sons said he drove until one time he was given a ticket and lost his license. He just never bothered to get it back, so his friends always drove him wherever he went. Sonny Brewer would drive four hours from Alabama to take William places such as Florida or Maine or the East Coast.

Shelia Kennedy, a true friend of William, would drive from Clarksville to Hohenwald, a two-hour trip, to take him to the Clarksville Writers' Conference. On one night of the conference every year, a book signing and banquet with a "big name" author would be held. Shelia knew that William was uncomfortable in large crowds, so she'd take him back to the hotel where he was staying as soon as he could leave the dinner. Each writer at the conference sat at a table with those who attended the affair as contributors or attendees of the conference. When William was introduced, he usually had already quietly left the building, so quietly that even those at his table were surprised that he was gone. Back at the hotel, Tom Franklin and William would spend a few hours together talking and imbibing their drink of choice, usually wine for Tom and beer or coffee for William.

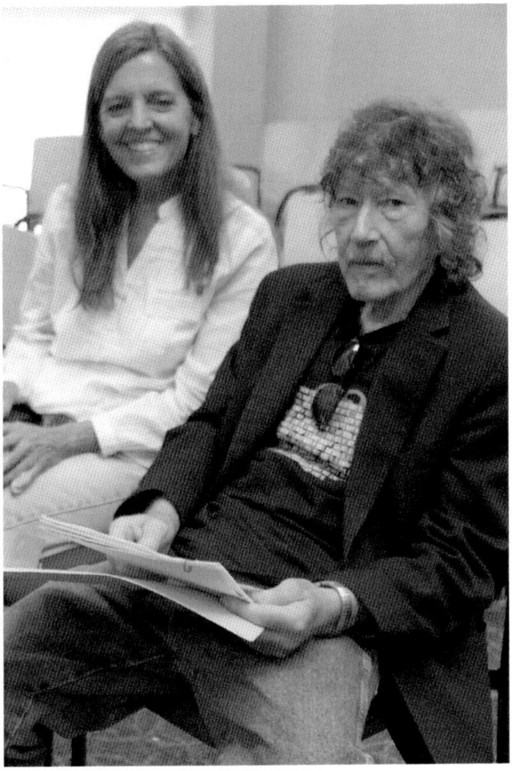

Shelia Kennedy waits with William Gay prior to reading. *Bill Larson.*

William had two heart attacks before the doctors insisted that he have a pacemaker. He didn't want to do it, but when they explained the consequences if he didn't, he acquiesced.

William had some bad luck with his work. His first novel, *The Lost Highway*, "went astray at the publishers." Another novel was stolen from his house. He said whoever stole it would never be able to publish it, though, because it wasn't written in sequence and there was no synopsis written yet. William wrote sentences from several compositions at the time and later put them together like a jigsaw puzzle that only he knew the answer to.

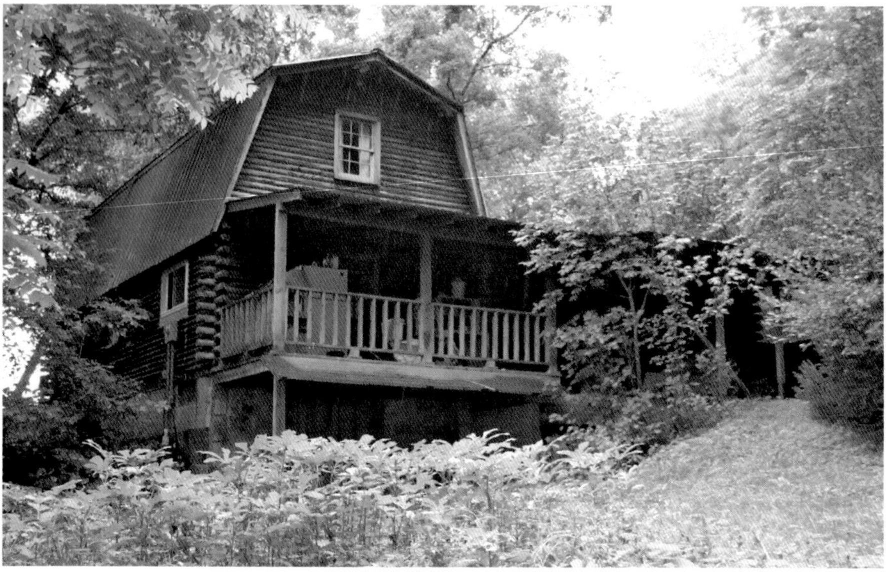

Side of William Gay's house. *Bill Larson.*

William didn't always answer the phone. In fact, he'd go many days at the time without answering the phone; this ended up causing great consternation among his friends. Various ones would try and try to reach him with no luck. Eventually, someone would either call one of his children or his brother or just drive up to his house to see about him. He'd be fine usually, just not in the mood to answer the phone.

His language was filled with the type of speech that he wrote; in other words, some of the words were not longer than four letters. He vowed never to get on another airplane after he had to sit with Tom Franklin for hours before takeoff on one in South Carolina because of some paperwork that didn't match a human organ in a cooler.

William wrote on either notebooks or yellow pads with ink. He could type but wasn't especially fast. When Shelia Kennedy found out that the dog had knocked a beer over into the keyboard of William's computer, she took her older one down for him to use. Sometimes other people typed his manuscripts for him. His handwriting was quite clear when he printed but was extremely tiny. If you asked him to autograph your book, he'd write, "To (person's name), from William."

He didn't bother with a cellphone or voice mail or caller ID.

William smoked continuously when he could but not where people would have a problem with it. He liked going to Oxford, Mississippi bars until they became

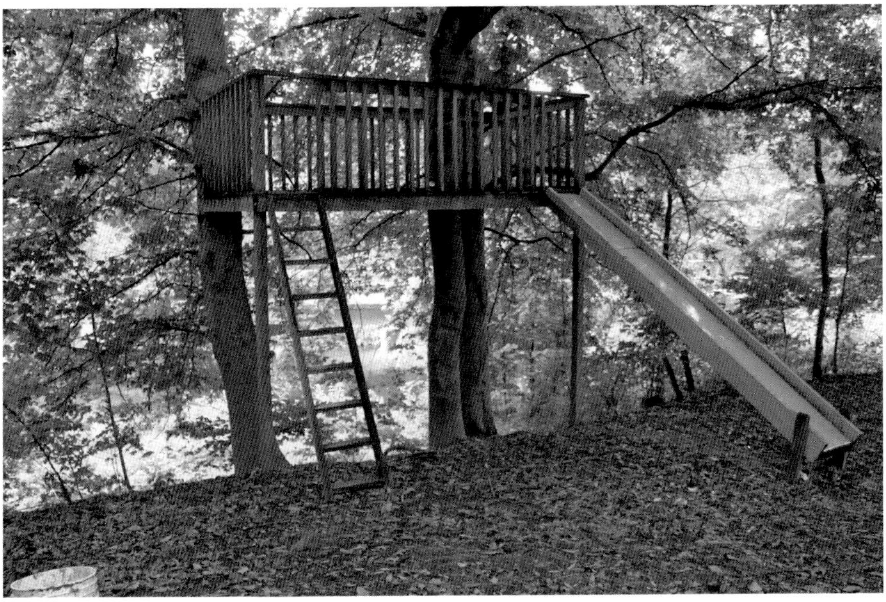

William Gay's treehouse in his front yard where he sometimes wrote. *Bill Larson.*

nonsmoking. He drank quite a bit, especially when he was around a lot of people because that would make him nervous, but when he was older, he drank only coffee at home. He'd drink some away from home because he was usually around a bunch of strangers and not comfortable with that kind of situation.

> *If my mind's bored, it tells me a story.*
>
> *William Gay*

William never comprehended his effect on other people. When he would speak to an English class or group of writers and whoever had invited him would try to impress on him how meaningful his presence had been, he'd say, "Really?" (Tom Franklin said William pronounced that word like "Israeli" without the "is.")

Once, when William read "The Paperhanger" to a group of students in Ohio, dead silence filled the room afterward. Tom Franklin, who had invited William, then learned that none of the Midwestern students could understand anything William said because of his Southern accent.

William chose his attire for readings from seeing John Prine in a concert. He said Prine had on a white shirt, jeans and a blue blazer, so from then on, that's what William always wore for public appearances.

When he read to audiences, he did not raise his voice. His quiet demeanor contrasted with some of the words he had written. He admitted that when his older daughter Lee began to read some of his work, it was difficult for her to imagine that her loving father could write such violence and mayhem.

He did not believe in wounding others or their feelings. If he did not care for someone's work, he would never write a critique for it. He believed that the opening of one's inner soul on the page of a manuscript was too personal for another to cause suffering.

A number of times, he told the story of a woman in his hometown who asked him who was helping him with his writing. William asked, "What do you mean by that?" And she said, "Well, I knew your family a long time, and they're not that smart. I knew you when you were younger, and you're not that smart. I was wondering if you had somebody who took out the little words and put in the big words." That was a wound that never healed and is possibly his basis for never making that kind of remark to another writer.

In 1999, William won the William Peden Award and the James A. Michener Memorial Prize. In 2002, he won a Guggenheim Fellowship and was named the 2007 U.S.A. Ford Foundation Fellow. United States Artists, a public charity that supports and promotes the work of American artists, granted William $50,000.

In 2007, Stephen King listed *Twilight* as the number one book on his most memorable books list. William said he read the list from bottom to top and was thoroughly surprised when he saw his book at the top—mainly because he had no idea that Stephen King would ever read his work.

During his last years, William began to show some of his paintings. When he took some to Landmark Booksellers in Franklin, he was astounded as a man walked in and bought every one of them before the show ever opened. He later had an exhibit at Southside Gallery in Oxford, Mississippi. His son Chris has two of his paintings; all the rest have been sold and are in private collections.

*Time Done Been Won't Be No More* was published by his good friend Michael White. It contains some of William's stories, essays, memoirs and reproductions of his paintings; it also contains the complete bibliography of his work. Michael used to arrive at William's house a few days before Christmas during his last years; he'd bring a turkey and the trimmings so that the family would have a good holiday. By then, between William's hospital bills and those of his daughter, the prize money was gone.

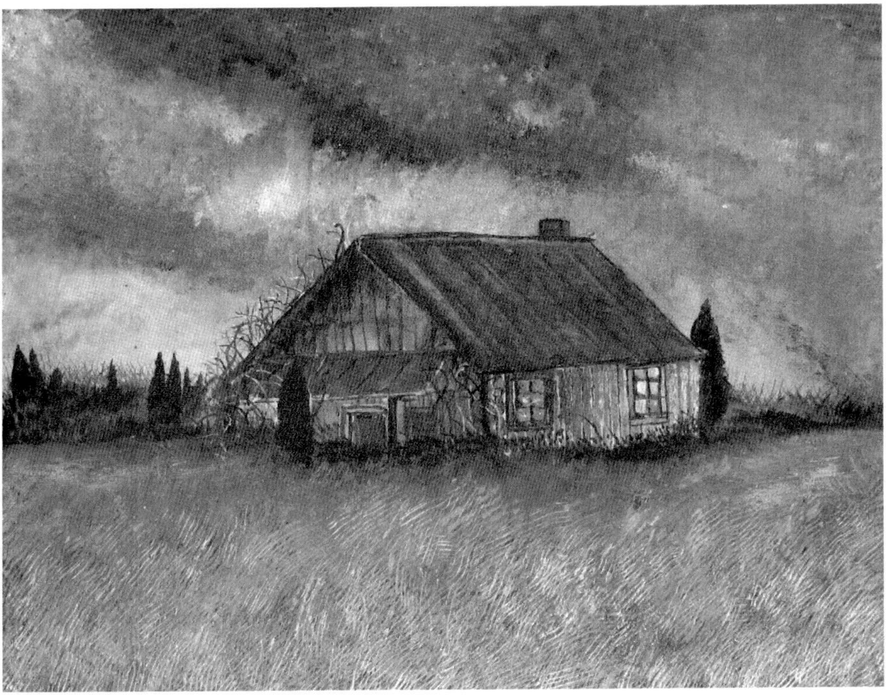

Painting by William Gay. *Photo by J.M. White.*

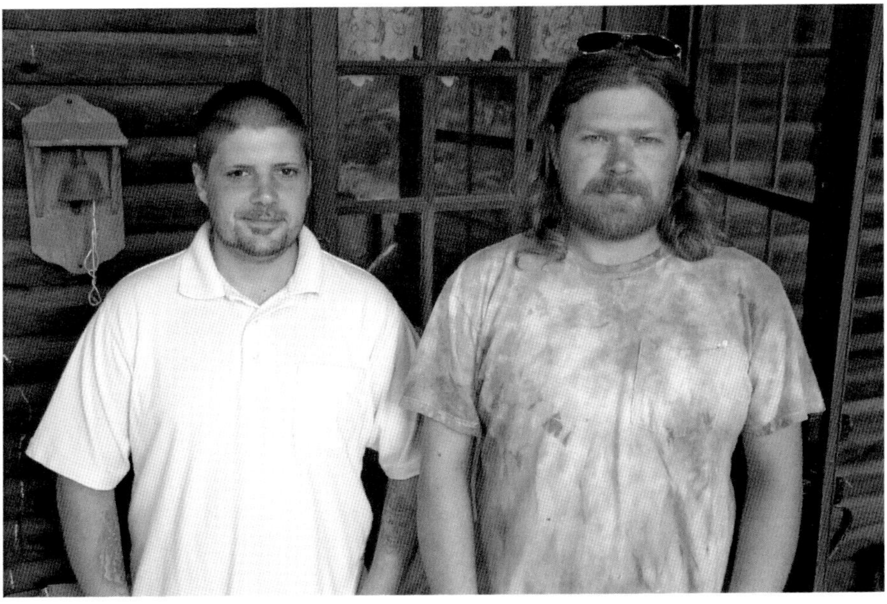

William's sons (left to right) William and Chris. *Bill Larson.*

## Death and Reflections of Friends

On the night of February 23, 2012, William made a fire in his wood-burning stove, according to his son Chris. Then he went into his bedroom, closed the door and died, apparently of a heart attack. He wanted no funeral and was cremated. Chris placed a headstone in the family cemetery but the ashes were scattered near the place where he was born.

It took many of the larger newspapers in the country a few days to learn that William had died, but eventually, the *New York Times*, the *Washington Post* and other newspapers ran extensive obituaries of the man whose name never became a household word. Yet the stories and novels he wrote will live forever in the annals of literature.

Tom Franklin and Marshall Chapman, both close friends of William, wrote moving tributes in the *Oxford American*.

Sonny Brewer marvels at the command of the English language William had. The phrase "A hot August sun was smoking up over a wavering tree line. Such drunks as were still about struggled beneath the malign heat slowly and painfully as if they moved in altered time or through an atmosphere thickening to amber" from *The Long Home* is but a small sample of William's art of description.

The name William Gay never hit the bestseller list, nor were his the books most people had on their bedside tables at night. That doesn't mean they shouldn't have been.

"I bet God has William Gay's books on his bedside table," said Karen Spears Zacharias in "The Brilliant Gay." Many writers and all his friends agree.

After William Gay died, I was able to buy an old notebook from his younger son; it had been found when the house was cleaned out. Here is a passage never published that gives a glimpse of William's need for writing:

> *Why you do it.*
>
> *I don't know. I don't question all my motives. Why does the wind blow, the little dog laugh to see such sport. It's just what I do. Why do people spend their entire lives in a factory making the same damn thing over and over, as if they never quite make it right.*
>
> *Well, people have to live.*
>
> *There you are then. I have to live.*
>
> *William Gay*

CHAPTER FIVE

# ALEX HALEY ON THE PATH OF FAMILY HISTORY

*The time would be just about as the dusk was deepening into the night, with the lightning bugs flickering on and off around the honeysuckle vines, and every evening I can remember, unless there was some local priority gossip, always they would talk about the same things—snatches and patches of what later I'd learn was the long, cumulative family narrative that had been passed down across the generations.*

*Alex Haley*

For the rest of the world, the two ultimate questions are "Who am I?" and "Why am I here?" But for the Southerner, the third question—"Who's your daddy?"—is bound to come up in the conversation. Tennessee writer Alex Haley started a national search for the answer to this question when he wrote *Roots*. The story of his own life revolves around a small town in West Tennessee called Henning.

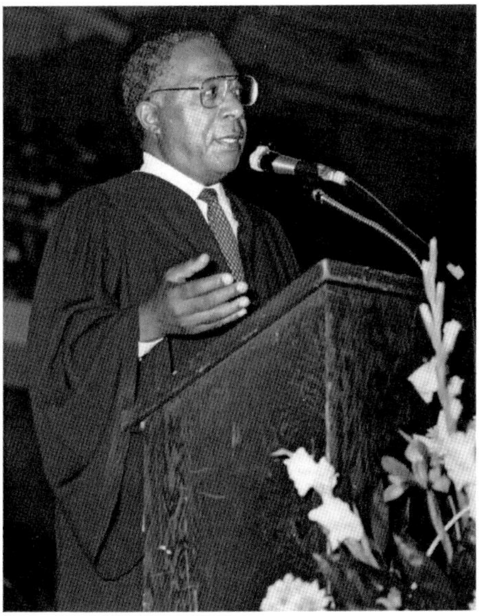

Alex Haley. *University Historian Collection, AR 0015, Box 76, University of Tennessee Libraries, Knoxville, Special Collections.*

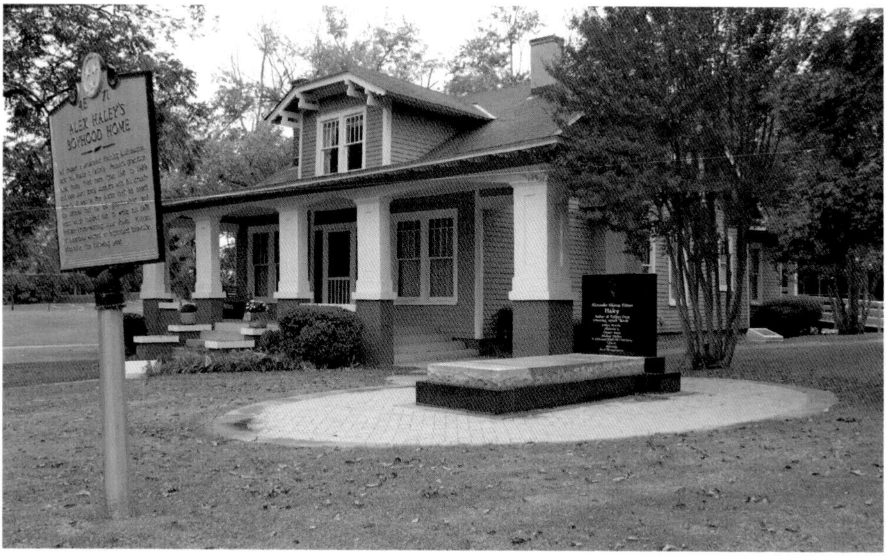


Home of Alex Haley's grandparents in Henning, location of Alex Haley's burial site. *Bill Larson.*

## EARLY LIFE

Alexander Murray Palmer Haley was born on August 11, 1921, in Ithaca, New York. His father, Simon Alexander Haley, was a college professor and his mother, Bertha George Palmer Haley, was a music teacher. When Alex was born, his father was a graduate student at Cornell University, where he was studying agriculture. Initially, Alex's mother moved him to her parents' home in Henning while his father finished his studies. At the end of that degree, his father then moved to Henning, too.

Alex was an intelligent child who managed to graduate from high school at age fifteen. He then went to Alcorn A&M College in Mississippi, where he did not distinguish himself according to all reports. After one year, he transferred to Elizabeth City State Teachers College in North Carolina but quit to join the Coast Guard; he was seventeen at the time.

## COAST GUARD SERVICE

Minorities were allowed to join the Coast Guard at that time in only two positions: mess attendant and steward's mate. Alex signed up for three years as a mess attendant third class on May 24, 1939. He was immediately assigned to a cutter, *Mendota*, based out of Norfolk, Virginia. The cutter was a 250-foot "Lake" class ship that had been in service only a few years; Alex was trained "on the job" by Coast Guard veterans.

Bored during the long patrols, Alex began writing to relatives and friends, sometimes as many as forty letters a week, using the portable typewriter he had bought. Then, shipmates began having Haley write letters for them—usually love letters back home—and he acquired rather admirable amounts of money for his efforts. With this success in mind, Alex began writing stories and articles for which he acquired a rather substantial pile of rejection slips, but he was able to have a few stories published and that kept him going.

At the same time, he was listening to the stories of the older sailors, most of whom had considerable experiences they were willing to share.

Alex Haley was transferred to an older cutter, *Pamlico*, which had been commissioned in 1907; its home port was New Bern, North Carolina. He was promoted to officer's steward third class on March 26, 1942, after the United States entered World War II.

On May 7, 1943, he was once again transferred to a large cargo vessel, the USS *Murzim* (AK-95). The ship was assigned to the Pacific Theater, where it was involved in extremely hazardous duty. Its sister ship, the USS *Serpens*, was destroyed at Guadalcanal while offloading cargo; this disaster involved the greatest loss of life in Coast Guard history. The death toll was 193 Coast Guardsmen, 56 U.S. Army soldiers, and 1 U.S. Public Health Service surgeon.

Alex Haley then began writing about combat and sold his first article, "In the Pacific," to the *Coast Guard* magazine for its February 1944 issue. The article described life on the ship as the guardsmen crossed the Pacific anticipating another invasion.

He also started a newspaper for the ship; a mimeographed tome, it was entitled *Seafarer*. His editorial "Mail Call" described the emotions of service people who received no mail from friends or family; it was reprinted in major newspapers throughout the United States.

Finally recognized for his journalistic efforts near the end of the war, he was promoted to editor of the *Outpost*, a Coast Guard periodical published at the Coast Guard's Personnel Separation Center. The Ships Editorial Association gave him a "commendable mention for his work in that capacity." He was next assigned as a reporter, eventually being promoted first to assistant editor and then to editor of the *Helmsman*, another Coast Guard publication. He was at that time working in the Third Coast Guard District's headquarters in

New York City. On June 29, 1949, he was promoted to journalist first class, at the rank of first class petty officer, and later that year, on December 16, he was promoted to chief journalist. He was to hold that rank until he retired with twenty years of service in 1959.

During his years in New York, Alex Haley constantly wrote articles for the *Coast Guard* magazine and began serving as the assistant to the public relations officer. He was awarded the American Defense Service Medal, along with Sea Clasp, World War II Victory Medal, National Defense Service Medal, Asiatic-Pacific Campaign Medal, European, African & Middle Eastern Campaign Medal, American Theater Campaign Medal, Korean Service Medal, Coast Guard Good Conduct Award (seven of these), the Commandant's Letter of Commendation, a rating of Expert Rifleman and an honorary degree from the Coast Guard Academy.

The Coast Guard named the USCGC *Alex Haley* for him on July 10, 1999. The cutter was originally based in Kodiak, Alaska.

## RELATIONSHIPS

*I'm just not a stationary husband.*
*Alex Haley*

Haley's private life involved his marriage to Nannie Branch in 1941; he met her in North Carolina when his ship was based there. Their marriage ended after thirteen years in 1954, after which he married Juliette Collins later that year. This marriage ended in 1972. His marriage to Dr. Myra Lewis (they met in Jamaica when she was twenty-six and he was fifty-two) occurred about 1977. This last marriage was somewhat of a secret, and he never introduced Myra to his children. After his death, it was learned that he had continued talking on the phone to his first wife, and she believed that they would eventually reconcile. The ensuing legal battle over Haley's estate is a story in itself.

## LIFE AS A FREELANCE WRITER

When Alex Haley left the Coast Guard, he moved to New York into a one-room basement apartment in Greenwich Village to devote himself to full-time writing. His halfhearted efforts at finding any kind of steady work failed, so he began writing sixteen to eighteen hours a day. He made friends with James Baldwin and C. Eric Lincoln, author of *The Black Muslims of America.*

Eventually, Haley sold stories to *Reader's Digest* and *This Week.* It was his *Playboy* interviews that led to a significant change in his career. He first interviewed jazz trumpet player Miles Davis. This was followed by interviews with Jim Brown, Cassius Clay (Mohammed Ali), Sammy Davis Jr., Quincy Jones and Leontyne Price. While working on these interviews, Haley also became notorious for missing deadlines on a regular basis.

It was when he interviewed Malcolm X and eventually worked with him for more than two years to write *The Autobiography of Malcolm X* that Haley became nationally known. The book was published in 1965, just two weeks before Malcolm X was shot; the book had an immense influence on the Nation of Islam (Black Muslim) movement. By 1977, *The Autobiography of Malcolm X* had sold more than six million copies around the world. Malcolm X had had a premonition that he would not live to see the book printed, and he was correct.

Haley asserted that the difference in the lives of Malcolm X and Martin Luther King Jr. hung by a thread. Malcolm X had been a pimp and a dope dealer in his early life but transformed himself into the leader of a powerful group of people. He believed that Islam was based on universal principles of brotherhood that rejected race as identity. By the end of his autobiography, Malcolm X had begun to reject the violence of Black Power movement and the Black Panthers as the road to civil rights; as a result, he was assassinated by those who wished to continue on that path. Martin Luther King Jr., on the other hand, chose to follow the path of Gandhi by using civil disobedience and rejecting violence in order to bring about rights for minorities.

*The Autobiography of Malcolm X* was chosen as one of the "Ten Best American Books of the 1960s Decade" and is still required reading in many schools.

After the book on Malcolm X was published, Haley said that he could easily make a minimum of $100,000 a year by writing articles for magazines and through speaking engagements.

> *To this day, people, particularly African American people but white people as well, will just totally, unexpectedly walk up and not say a word, just walk up and hug you and then say, "Thank you."*
>
> *Alex Haley, in a radio interview just before his death*

## *Roots*

In 1965, Haley began researching post–Civil War records in the National Archives in Washington, D.C. He accidentally came across the names of his maternal great-grandparents. Later, when researching in the British Museum, he saw the Rosetta Stone that had unlocked the secret of Egyptian hieroglyphs. This stimulated Haley's thinking in terms of deciphering the unknown history of his family, a journey that took eleven years and created an interest in genealogy in the United States that became almost a frenzy. Haley even took an ocean voyage from Liberia to the United States as part of his research; he spent his nights lying on a board in the hold of the ship while wearing only his underwear to feel the type of conditions a slave might have experienced.

Alex Haley went to Juffure, a village in The Gambia, West Africa, to see if he could trace his ancestor as described through the family history he had been hearing on the front steps of his grandparents' home since he was a child. He met Keebe Kanji Fofana, the old native griot (oral historian), who told him that his ancestor Kunta Kinte was captured as a slave there. (Some doubters claim that the old man was a well-known trickster who was feeding Haley just what he wanted to hear.)

*Roots*, published in 1976, traced Haley's family from 1750. Originally promoted as nonfiction, the resulting criticisms and lawsuits forced it to be reclassified as fiction. However, *Roots* took the world by storm. In 1977, it gleaned the National Book Award, the Spingarn Medal (given by the National Association for the Advancement of Colored People [NAACP] annually for outstanding achievement by an African American) and a special Pulitzer Prize.

Made into a television miniseries that ran from January 23 to January 30, 1977, it was seen by 130 million viewers, the largest television audience up to that time. The miniseries featured Ed Asner, Chuck Connors, Carolyn Jones, O.J. Simpson, Ralph Waite, Louis Gossett Jr., Lorne Greene, Robert Reed, LeVar Burton (who portrayed Kunta Kinte), Ben Vereen (Chicken George), Lynda Day George, Vic Morrow, Raymond St. Jacques, Sandy Duncan, John Amos, Leslie Uggams, Cicely Tyson, MacDonald Carey, George Hamilton, Ian MacShane, Richard Roundtree, Lloyd Bridges, Doug McClure, Maya Angelou and Burl Ives, to name a few.

A later television series, *Roots: The Next Generations*, was produced in 1979. This series had six episodes, unlike the eight of the first series. It encompassed the period from 1882 to the 1970s.

"Who's your daddy?" became a national search for the family history of people of all ethic groups. African Americans could look to the book as evidence that it was indeed possible to trace one's history even if slavery had been part of that legacy.

> *My image is important to me, and I can never get it back if I lose it.*
>
> *Alex Haley to his third wife, Myra*

## LEGAL PROBLEMS

With no good deed going unpunished, Alex Haley was sued three times over *Roots*. Margaret Walker Alexander contended that he had plagiarized her novel, *Jubilee*. This lawsuit was dismissed because the allegations were not proved.

In 1978, Leonard S. Brown Jr. sued Alex Haley, Warner Brothers and at least eighteen other prominent persons for numerous offenses; completely without merit, the suit never went to trial.

Most serious of the claims against Haley was of plagiarism that was contended by Harold Courlander for about eighty instances in *The African* published in 1967. Haley eventually admitted two short passages had found their way into *Roots* and settled the case out of court for $650,000, a large portion of which was paid by Doubleday, the publisher, according to records in Special Collections, the University of Tennessee.

The University of Tennessee has extensive collections of the Haley papers for anyone wishing to learn more details of his writing and life.

## AFTER *ROOTS*

After having had numerous honorary degrees granted to him and extensive publicity, notoriety and fame, Alex Haley's next book to be published (in 1988) was *A Different Kind of Christmas*. This book describes the life of a son of a Southern plantation owner who had an extensive holding of slaves to work his fields. The son goes to a Northern college where he learns from Quaker classmates of the Underground Railroad and decides that slavery is inherently evil. He becomes one of the agents and becomes involved in a plot to free the slaves of his own parents on a trip home for Christmas.

Haley worked periodically on a musical eventually called *The Way* that described how interracial struggles were an inanity. He also started many other projects, such as *Henning*, a book on his hometown, that was published after his death. Additionally, he started several television and movie scripts, but most were not preserved.

In 1991, Haley gave extensive records of his work to the University of Tennessee and planned to assist in their organization; this was not to occur due to his untimely death.

On February 10, 1992, Alex Haley died of a heart attack at age seventy just prior to a planned speaking engagement in Seattle, Washington.

After Haley's death, *Queen*, the story of his father's family, was published in 1993 by William Morrow and Company. It also was made into a miniseries starring Halle Berry, Ann-Margret, Patricia Clarkson and Tim Daley.

It was discovered after his death that he owed between $1.5 and $2 million, including about $100,000 in personal debts, to various creditors. His brother, George, an attorney, was appointed executor of the will. All ten of Alex Haley's Tennessee properties were mortgaged, so George auctioned all of his brother's literary material, including notes, manuscripts and research items from both *Roots* and *The Autobiography of Malcolm X*. Even the Pulitzer Prize and all Alex Haley's personal items—

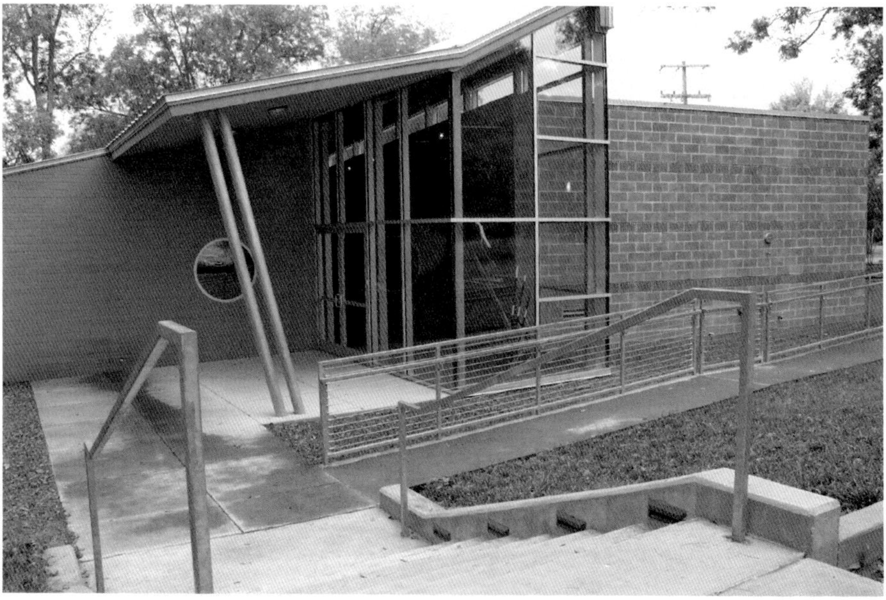

Alex Haley Interpretive Center in Henning. *Bill Larson*.

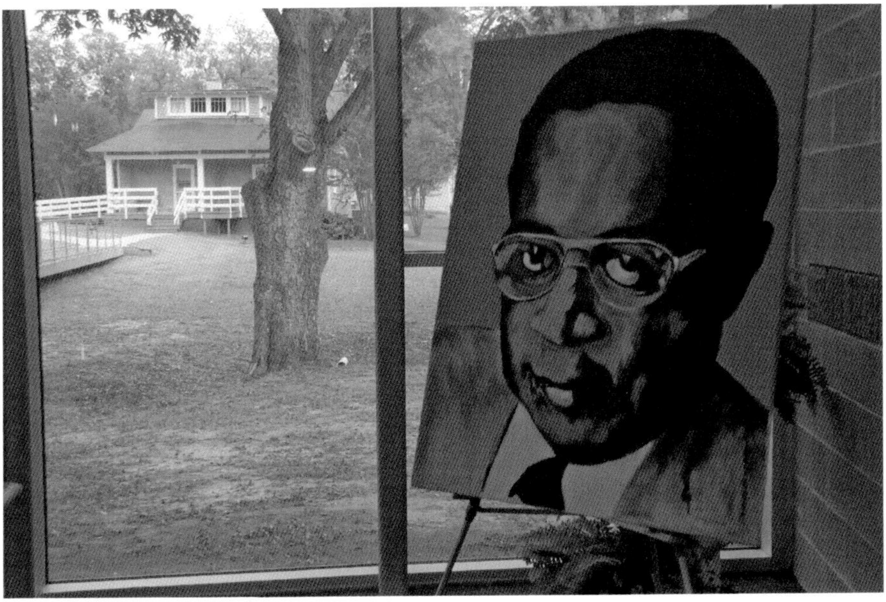

Alex Haley portrait, donated by Jerry Johnson in 2007, with Alex Haley Museum in background. *Bill Larson.*

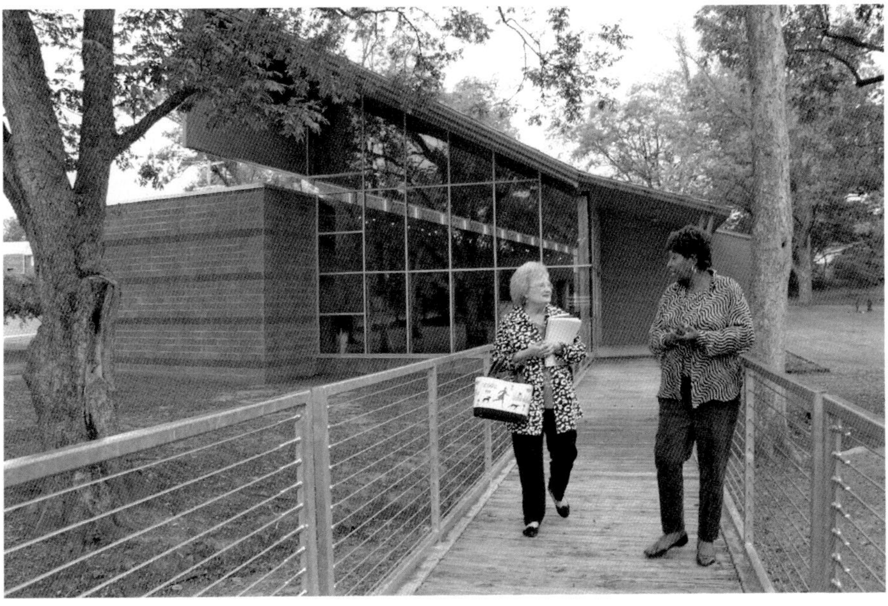

Beverly Johnson and I on bridge to Haley Museum. *Bill Larson.*

memorabilia, antiques, awards, furniture—were auctioned in order to keep the real estate from going into foreclosure. It was at this auction that the University of Tennessee, bidding against people from all over the world both in person and on the phone, was able to acquire another significant amount of Haley's work. No manuscript was sold intact but was parceled in sections instead, which increased the amount of sales. It is estimated that the three-day auction raised about $800,000.

An extensive description of the aftermath of Haley's death was written by Terry Greene in the *Phoenix New Times* on November 11, 1992; it can be found online.

Alex Haley is buried at his boyhood home in Henning, Tennessee. The house is now the Alex Haley Museum and Interpretive Center and was listed on the National Register of Historic Places on December 14, 1978. Restored with some of the 1919 furniture from the original family home, the house is open Tuesday through Saturday from 10:00 a.m. to 5:00 p.m. It was originally constructed by Alex Haley's grandfather Will E. Palmer during 1918 and 1919. Tours can be scheduled by calling 731-738-2240 and speaking to Paula Boger, Director.

CHAPTER SIX

# VIETNAM VETERAN BUD WILLIS REVEALS A HUEY PILOT'S WAR

Author and Tennessee native Bud Willis was awarded the 2012 Distinguished Arts and Humanities Medal for Literary Arts in Memphis on November 9, 2012. This honor was formerly bestowed on John Grisham, Eudora Welty, Shelby Foote and other luminaries in the world of literature.

Bud's family has a long history of service to the United States dating back to the Revolutionary War.

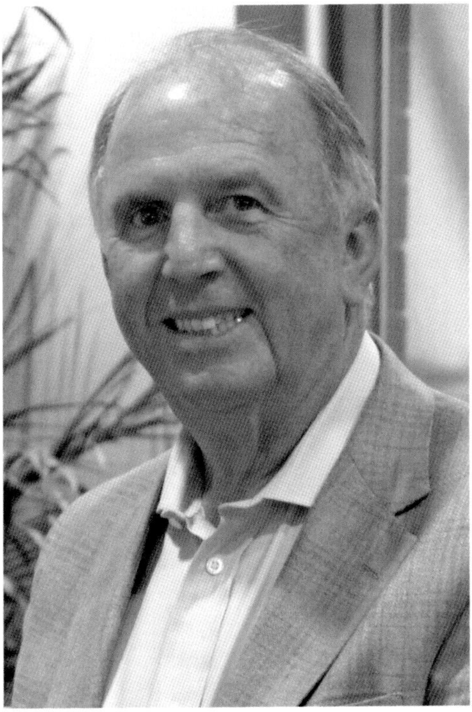

Beasley "Bud" Willis. *Courtesy of Bud and Lee Willis.*

## FAMILY CONNECTIONS

Captain Daniel McKissick, Bud's four times great-grandfather, lost an arm at the Battle of Ramsour's Mill in North Carolina in 1780, when he was struck by a British musket ball. Promoted to the rank of colonel, McKissick was sent to chart the city of Shelbyville, Tennessee, the county seat of Bedford County. On July 4, 1810, he sold the original lots on the town square, purchasing one hundred acres for himself near Bluestocking Hollow, which became the home where Bud's mother, Margaret Louise Dryden, was born and raised. Margaret was related to Daniel McKissick through her mother, Emma Mae White.

John Harlan Willis, of nearby Columbia, Tennessee, the nephew of Bud's father, Pete, was one of eight Tennesseans to receive the Medal of Honor (MOH) during World War II. Pharmacist Mate Willis, a corpsman attached to the marine unit during the Battle of Iwo Jima, was wounded while aiding wounded Marines near Japanese-held Hill 362. After being ordered back to the battle-aid station, he returned to assist other marines. When the enemy began attacking with hand grenades. Willis threw back eight live grenades before being mortally wounded when the ninth exploded in his hand. Marines who witnessed this rallied to seize the victory with hand-to-hand combat and gave credit to Willis for the victory. Twenty-eight monuments were named in his honor, including the destroyer escort USS *John Willis* (DE-1027) and the gates of Millington Naval Air Station in Memphis.

Margaret Louise Dryden married Burr (called "Pete") Willis in 1929 in Shelbyville near Bluestocking. Pete was an alcoholic and abusive father and, after fathering nine children, eventually left home in 1947 after a confrontation with the couple's oldest son, Horace, age sixteen. With the other children huddled in the front room, Horace had had enough of seeing his mother's mistreatment and made it physically clear that Pete was to sober up or leave them alone.

Bud's memoir, *Bluestocking*, chronicles his mother's courage and determination in rearing her nine children to be self-reliant and successful with whatever resources they could scrape together. Within a month of her husband's departure, Margaret and her children were evicted from their rental house, owned by a bootlegger friend of Pete. Margaret's youngest child was six weeks old at the time. Horace had to drop out of school and found work at the local newspaper, the *Tullahoma News*.

With community help, the family moved into a tiny house behind a "filling station," where they lived for the next two years, from 1947 to the summer of 1949. Every child did as much as possible to help the family keep food on the table and heat in the house during winter. Ten-year-old Sara sold newspapers for a nickel each because she could keep half the money. Other children worked at a lemonade stand, raking leaves, mowing lawns and babysitting, and later, the older girls, Martha and Ann, worked at Davis's Department Store. Young Tommy, fourth in the brood, eventually found a job at the pool hall. "Buddy" (as Bud, whose birth name was "Beasley," was called by everyone in the family) eventually sold newspapers for many years and honed his skills as a salesman. Returning soft drink bottles for a penny each became a source of income. Occasionally, free samples of cereal or other foods were available, and those items found their way into Willis's stomach as well. On a school free lunch program, Bud was happy to have the cold milk and graham crackers provided when he reached school because, for years, his family did not own a refrigerator.

> *Laziness is poverty's biggest challenge. You have to fight it every day, or it will set in like* rigor mortis. *But if you keep your feet moving and the energy flowing, you can give serendipity a chance to make something happen.*
>
> *Bud Willis,* Bluestocking

Margaret Willis bought food on Friday nights, if anyone had a paycheck that week, and would not accept government assistance for groceries. Her typical grocery list included ten pounds of potatoes, dried pinto beans, powdered milk, bread, canned tomatoes, corn meal, macaroni and margarine. Of course, the family had a garden in the summer, and they grew corn, tomatoes, okra, squash, green onions and field peas.

Their intrepid mother became an excellent seamstress and not only made prom and party dresses but took in alterations as well. Buddy's Robin Hood costume helped make him a star in the school play.

> *Mama never laid a hand on me. The way she corrected her children was by saying something subtle like, "Let's make sure we never have to go through anything like that again." The way she showed her love was by being there. Every second of every minute of every hour of every day, Mama was right there for us, twenty-four seven.*
>
> *Bud Willis,* Bluestocking

Bud reveals not only his life but also those of his eight brothers and sisters as they grew up in Tullahoma. His sisters were popular in high school, and the oldest girls were crowned Miss Tullahoma. Bud worked small jobs late into the night, at the same time participating in high school sports, where he was captain of the football and basketball team. At the first football game she attended, Margaret overheard some local fans commenting loudly that Bud dropped a pass he should have caught. On the next play, Mrs. Willis yelled out, "Don't throw it to Willis!" much to the amusement of her children who knew this was strictly out of character for her.

Bud went by the name Buddy until he reached college at Tennessee Tech. As a freshman, he met a beautiful redhead when he accidentally found himself in the "ladies' room" rather than the "men's room." When he asked her to go out with him, she told him that her dog was named "Buddy," so she certainly couldn't date anyone by that name. They settled on "Bud," and that's the name that stuck, except for during his days as a pilot in Vietnam, where he was nicknamed "Boo Radley" for Harper Lee's mysterious character in *To Kill a Mockingbird.*

## DREAMS OF BEING A WRITER

Bud's interest in a writing career began in seventh grade when his teacher Ms. Hill assigned a story to be written by each member of the class each week. The story had to involve all twenty-five vocabulary words for the week. Taking a clue from the cowboy serial movies he saw at the local theater every Saturday, Bud began his own serial that involved a couple of bumbling burglars who always failed in their lives of crime. The other kids in the class couldn't wait for the next hilarious installment. Buoyed by their acceptance, the feeling of success and its accompanying power, Bud knew then that he wanted to become a writer.

At Tennessee Tech, Bud was named the editor of the campus literary magazine.

Bud Willis's books always reveal his unfailing sense of humor. Never self-aggrandizing, he gives credit where credit is due, not only to the members of his family but also to other individuals. That is not to say that he is flippant with details. Any book he writes will require a number of handkerchiefs, as he relates not only successes but also disappointments and even untimely death.

His philosophy and code of values are ever present.

*When I reflect back on all the times that I experienced problems in my life, there seemed to be one common denominator. I was taking myself far too seriously.*
*Bud Willis,* Bluestocking

## NOW A MARINE

While at Tennessee Tech, Bud was recruited for the marines by the football team quarterback, the president of the student body and the commander of the ROTC drill team. He claimed they were "looking for a few good men" to become marine officers and had chosen him to join them.

*When you grow up in Tennessee, you are likely to be taught the Pledge of Allegiance before you learn the Lord's Prayer. That's just how we roll.*
*Bud Willis,* Marble Mountain

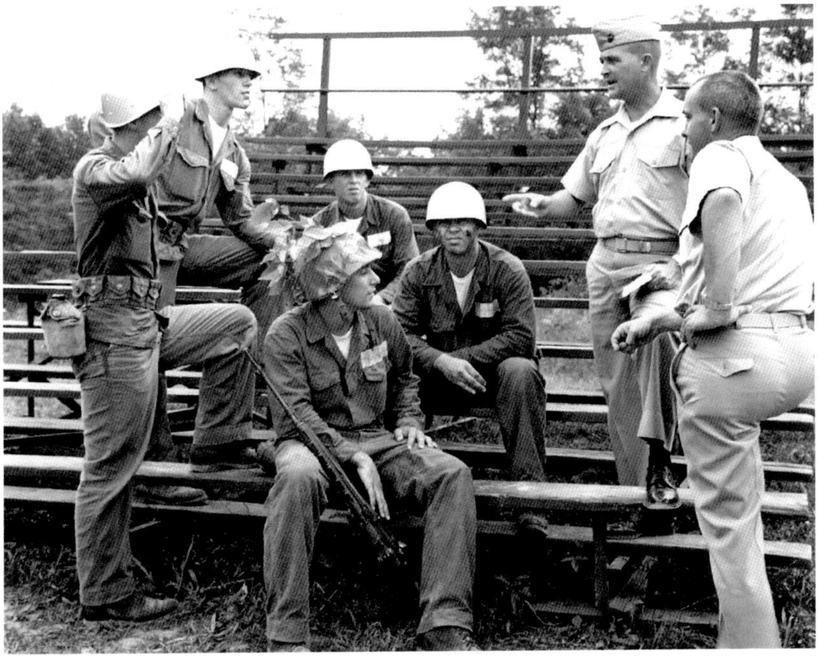

Bud Willis and fellow marines. *Courtesy of Bud and Lee Willis.*

Bud Willis's outstanding Vietnam memoir, *Marble Mountain*, is the result of his experiences as a Huey helicopter pilot near Danang, Vietnam.

> *I believe that there are ordinary people on this earth who possess a second, deeper intellect: an innate ability to anticipate the future and to steel their resolve and moral obligation to their duty. This is a contract that is born into them, and they are instinctively driven to action.*
>
> *Bud Willis,* Bluestocking

The people of Vietnam, Bud writes, believe they are descended from an ancient dragon. They also believe that the umbilical cord is the exact center of man, "where earth meets the sky." The center of Vietnam is Marble Mountain, about four kilometers from Danang. From the center of this ancient country, the U.S. Marine Corps had chosen to locate the helicopter facility for the pilots of Marine Air Group Sixteen and attempted to dominate the sky while hundreds of thousands of North Vietnamese soldiers invaded by land. Marble Mountain is where twenty-four-year-old Bud Willis found himself assigned for his thirteen-month tour during the longest war in American history.

Bud asserts that the thousands of Vietnamese had the advantage when invading by land, but it was in the air that the U.S. Marines dominated. Although two million Vietnamese died and the United States fought in Vietnam for fifteen years, in the end Ho Chi Minh's statement, "They will kill many of us, and we will kill a few of them, and they will grow tired of it," rang true.

Bud Willis wrote *Marble Mountain: A Vietnam Memoir* when he was sixty-eight years old. The book resulted from the letters he wrote home and a journal he kept throughout his tour of duty in 1966.

When he left Tennessee to serve in Vietnam, Bud was married to Kay Fleming Willis from Columbus, Mississippi, and they had a two-week-old son, Kirk McGuire Willis. They later had a second son, Kevin Dryden Willis, in 1969. Eventually, Kay and Bud divorced. "When [I] came home from that war, we were not the same," he admits. Divorce is just one more sad statistic for deployed soldiers.

In 2002, Bud married Susan Lee Barnes, a real estate broker from Columbia, Kentucky. Now retired, Bud and Lee live in Naples, Florida, with their Coton de Tulear, Boo, who is trained as a PAWS therapy dog to work with hospice patients.

He talks in *Marble Mountain* about trying to watch *Apocalypse Now* alone; it took five times for him to be able to sit through the entire movie. "The fear

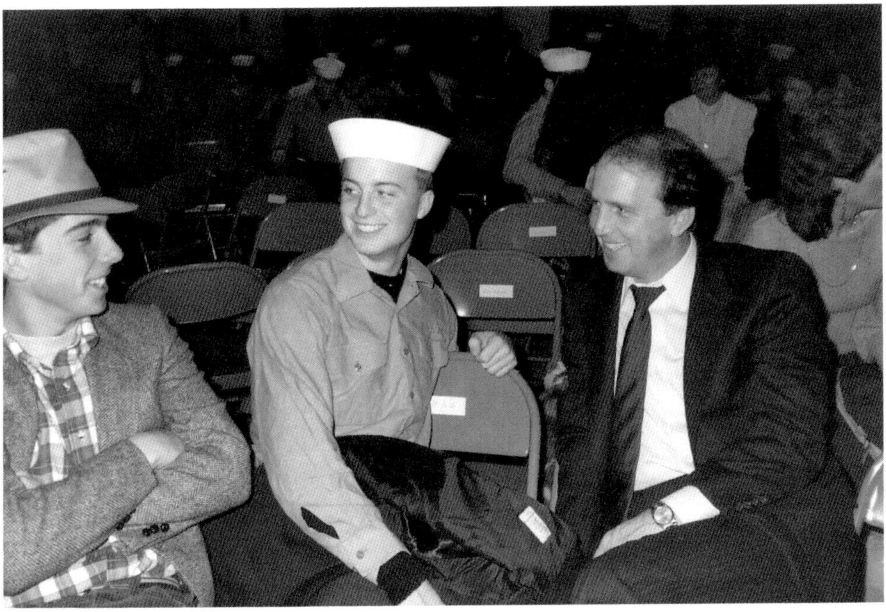

*Above*: Bud Willis and his sons, Kirk and Kevin, at Kirk's graduation from basic training in the navy. *Courtesy of Bud and Lee Willis.*

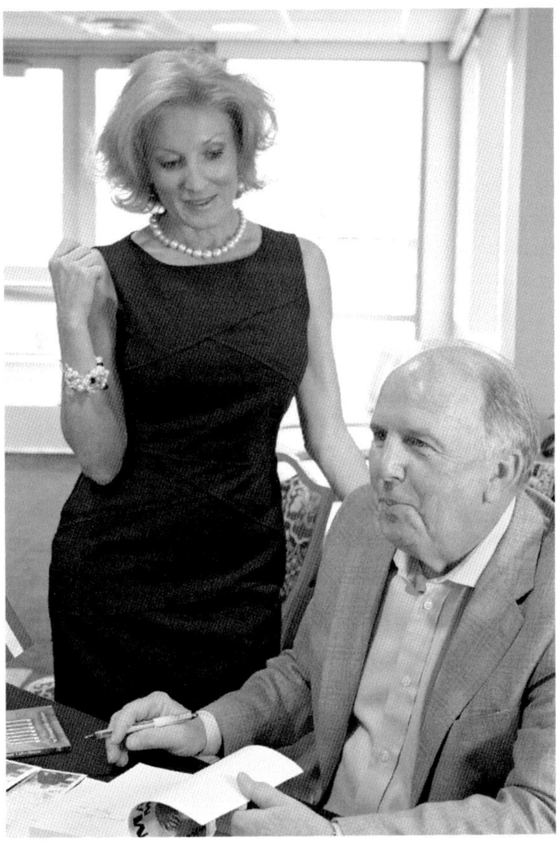

*Right*: Lee and Bud Willis at a book signing. *Bill Larson.*

factor of combat was so intense that I couldn't process it all in one sitting," he said.

*Marble Mountain* is really a "coming of age story" and is not intended to be a military book, according to Bud. He takes the reader through the developing inner drama of a youngster who is confronted with the daily fear of death and grows to become a seasoned pilot who devotes himself to the marines on the ground who are facing an enemy that chains its soldiers to weapons and has little respect for individual human life. Bud does not try to paint himself as a hero, but rather, he exalts the bravery of all the chopper pilots and especially the wounded young infantry soldiers they were sent to rescue.

*Marble Mountain* is a realistic look at what that war was about. Bud's descriptions of the struggle for power and control of the rice fields of Southeast Asia contrast with the political positions of the time, but as he points out, things are rarely as they seem to be, especially where politics is concerned. He paints an accurate picture of how experience, not rank, in combat develops its own pecking order, as young lieutenants are allowed to command the aircraft while senior officers fly as their copilots into battle. It is not always a pretty picture.

Preparing for life as a helicopter pilot back in Pensacola, Florida, right after college, Bud heard the orientation talk that announced, "Only two of you will graduate from flight school. Of the two who become pilots, one of you will be killed before your tour of duty is up. That will leave only one of you standing. Are you sure you still want to become pilots?" Of course, the only answer was, "Yes, sir."

Each potential pilot was given a dozen flights with an instructor, and then he had to fly solo. Bud landed correctly the first time, but his first roommate took four tries and left the program that same night.

Pilots studied physics, engines, aerodynamics, flight theory, navigation and hydraulics and worked in flight simulators to learn complicated instrument procedures and methods for bad weather landings. They faced simulated altitudes of up to thirty thousand feet to experience oxygen deprivation, and they packed their own parachutes.

In 1965, Bud was transferred to the New River Air Facility at Jacksonville, North Carolina. Flying a Cessna C-170, the throttle stuck wide open during his first flight. He had to call "May Day" and circle the field until the fuel was gone. Landing perfectly next to the fire truck on the airfield, Bud was sure that his career was ended. Instead, all of the planes had to be grounded until the cause of the problem was determined, and Bud was commended for his handling of the problem. His training continued.

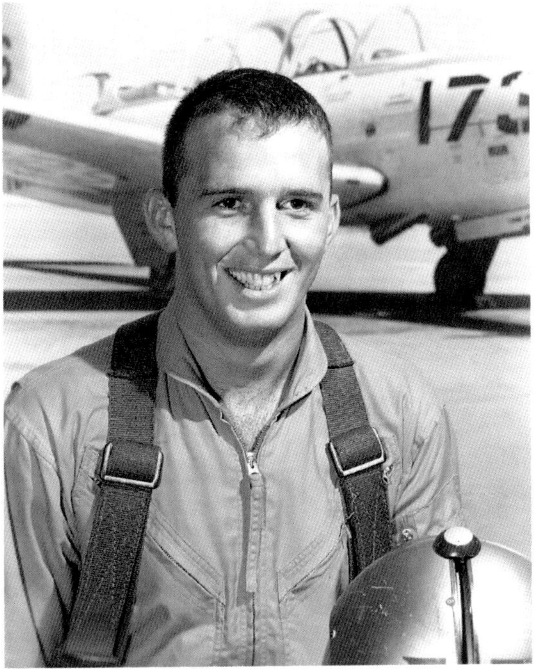

Bud Willis prepares for war. *Courtesy of Bud and Lee Willis.*

*Marble Mountain* begins with an incident in which Bud was shot down over a rice field; obviously, he survived the crash, but his book then eases the reader into the world of the helicopter pilot. Every day was an adventure of one sort or another.

The men who had been at Marble Mountain were tanned and thin from the eternal heat and daily stress. When Bud and the other pilots arrived, they had no assignments, not even for a place to sleep that night. They had to find a bunk vacated by a pilot on assignment.

The "hooch" (wooden-framed tent where pilots resided) was similar to a crude Quonset hut. It had plywood floors and brown tarps on the tops and sides. Cots were made of canvas and had uncomfortable mattresses. Some had blown-up rubber air mattresses with layers of green wool blankets between the sheets and the hot rubber. These narrow beds did not allow for tossing and turning—just for lying down, sleeping and waking. Between the beds was a bookcase or piece of paneling to provide a bit of privacy for each officer. Needless to say, it was not the Ritz.

> *The sand finds its way into everything: our ears, our shoes, our watchbands, our food, our teeth, and our "you-name-it." Sea water is not warm in the morning for bathing, and a bar of soap in salt water is like bathing with a piece of sandstone. A mouthful of the China Sea tastes similar to alum. A beach without females is no beach at all.*
>
> *Bud Willis,* Marble Mountain

A truck came by every night to spray insecticide to keep down the mosquitoes and flies. No running water or hot water was available in the shower, which consisted of a painted black fifty-five-gallon drum suspended overhead. Each person had a metal bowl for shaving and brushing teeth; water was fetched from a water truck and carried back to the hooch in a five-gallon can.

"Entertainment" (drinks with ice) was available initially in a tiki hut with a straw roof; it was open from early in the afternoon until lights out.

A five-foot-deep bunker lined with burlap sandbags stacked on top of each other was located between or under the hooches; these were available for the times when mortar attacks threatened the Marble Mountain residents. A generator provided electricity to the huts, except for when it was temporarily broken. Then the officers used flashlights—except for Bud, who initially didn't own one. As other pilots would leave to go home, basic equipment could be negotiated from the guys who no longer needed it.

The sheets on the bed where Bud initially had to sleep had not been washed in some time. When he finally was assigned a day off, that was one of his first priorities.

Food in the mess hall, he wrote, was good—no real milk, dehydrated eggs and no soft drinks but plenty of fresh vegetables and meat. Amazingly, no rice was served, even though, in Bud's opinion, the war was being fought over control of the rice fields and Marble Mountain was surrounded by them.

After a while, each day became another day without a name, except for Monday, when everyone took his malaria pill.

Almost every guy at Marble Mountain, including the commanding officers, had a nickname. Bud's nickname, Boo Radley, was written on the back of his helmet when he returned from R&R in Tokyo. After a general addressed him as Lieutenant Radley, he knew he'd never be Beasley Willis again.

*Marble Mountain* is, of course, about the missions that Bud and the other pilots carried out night and day. Bud flew 640 combat missions and was decorated thirty-two times with air medals. The majority of his book is devoted to the other pilots with whom he worked and the feats they accomplished.

> *One thing that is becoming clear to me is how important it is to fly as often as possible…Confidence is the key, and the only way to get it is to have as much information and experience as you can. Lady Luck doesn't hang out with the unprepared. Armed with experience, you can make better decisions and also justify your actions if necessary.*
>
> *Bud Willis,* Marble Mountain

Not to be missed is Bud's description of his riding through the wall of fear as he no longer rode copilot and took command as flight leader. His chapter "Epiphany" describes landing on the side of a hill, always a difficult feat, with enemy fire all around. Circling and stalling to gather a plan that would avoid harm to the men both in the helicopter and wounded on the ground—whom they were picking up—Bud knew that it would soon be dark. Suddenly, he leaned forward in his seat and made the call to go in as he stepped through the wall of fear. He describes this as his defining moment; he devoted his life to those young marines in a brotherhood of which he became a member, and he never looked back.

> *After you've picked up a few dead marines, everything fades into an assignment. The Marines are a family, and we have to look after our own.*
>
> *Bud Willis,* Marble Mountain

*Marble Mountain* follows Bud's career throughout his thirteen-month tour. It does nothing to glamorize war, nor does it gloss over the anxieties of being there. Even as his tour ends, Bud goes to sleep at night by feeling to make sure his arms and legs are still intact. The ride home is surreal, as the transition from imminent danger seems too good to be true.

This is not a book to be missed. A significant portion of all sales is donated to the Wounded Warrior Project.

## COMING HOME

Bud's next thirty-four years were spent as a broker and manager for J.C. Bradford & Company (and, later, companies that bought it out). He was named Outstanding Young Man for Tennessee for service to his community, state and country. He worked in Columbus, Mississippi; Clarksville and Memphis, Tennessee; Columbus and Cleveland, Ohio; and in Pensacola, Florida.

In 1995, he received the Community Involvement Award at the J.C. Bradford & Company Leadership Convention. He also served as chairman of the committee to commission a billion-dollar warship, the USS *Mitscher*, while he was working in Pensacola.

On November 13, 2008, Bud and Lee appeared on the NBC *Today Show* with Hoda Kotb and Kathie Lee Gifford in a segment called "Everyone Has a Story." Selected by a panel of judges as one of eight best of the thousands

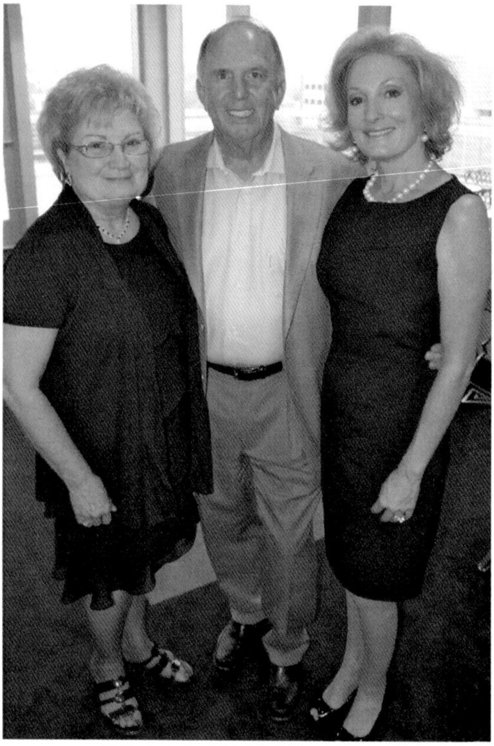

Me with Bud and Lee Willis. *Bill Larson.*

of entries, Bud's description of a young combat marine who was picked up after he had lost a leg, an arm, an eye and an ear for transport to the hospital, left no eye dry. The marine had sent a message to the pilot, "Thanks for the ride." Bud said that this incident reminded him to never let a day go by for the rest of his life that he didn't thank those who helped him along the way.

Bud Willis continues to speak to audiences throughout the country on the issues that confront young people as they serve their country through the U.S. military forces. His life of service is one of honor and self-sacrifice; he is an inspiration for all.

CHAPTER SEVEN

# ALICE RANDALL

## *BOUNTIFUL WRITER AND RENAISSANCE WOMAN*

Harvard-educated Alice Randall is as close to being a Renaissance woman as you're going to meet on the streets of Nashville.

Writer-in-residence for Vanderbilt University, she is the author of *The Wind Done Gone* (a winner of the 2001 Al Neuharth Free Spirit Award and on the bestseller list for six weeks, peaking at number nine). The family of Margaret Mitchell sued her publisher to block publication of the book; this resulted in a high-profile lawsuit that created arguments concerning parody, freedom of speech, censorship and copyright law. An out-of-court settlement allowed the book to be published; the publisher, Houghton Mifflin, also made a financial donation to Morehouse College, long supported by the Mitchell estate.

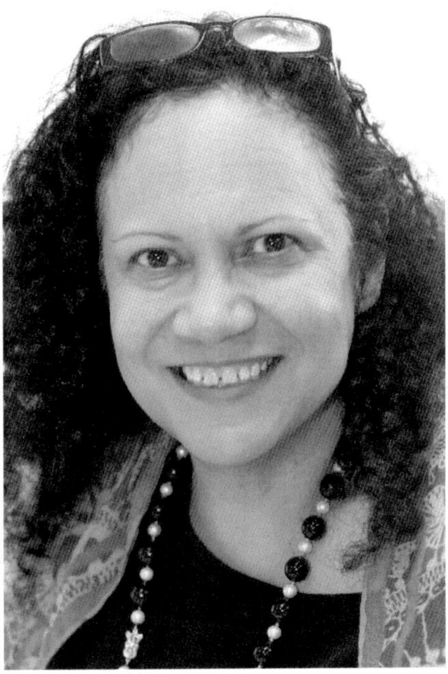

Alice Randall. *Bill Larson.*

Alice Randall has been quoted as feeling that her own book "unites the nation" because of the way African Americans are portrayed in Margaret

Mitchell's book. She believes that blacks are portrayed by Mitchell as intellectually inferior. Alice asserts that writing *The Wind Done Gone* is an act of love for her daughter, "so that she would not have to live her life with that text unanswered."

Her central character, Cynara, is the mulatto child of Mammy and Scarlett O'Hara's plantation-owner father. Cynara later becomes the mistress of Rhett Butler, who teaches her to write; she chronicles her life as a slave and concubine in a diary.

## After Controversy

Randall's other books are *Pushkin and the Queen of Spades*, *Rebel Yell* and, her latest book, *Ada's Rules*. Randall's second book, *Pushkin and the Queen of Spades*, won the Outstanding Fiction Award from the First Annual Mixed Media Watch Image Awards and also won honorable mention at the 2004 Myers Outstanding Book Awards.

*Rebel Yell* centers on Abel Jones Jr., the son of a famous black civil rights lawyer. Alice reminds readers that Abel, of course, was the first person in the Bible to be murdered, which is why she named her character that. She describes him as "colored-baby royalty," but he later dies while dining with his second wife, a white woman, at a dinner theater named Rebel Yell. When his first wife, Hope, learns about some of Abel's activities that might include CIA operations, she is haunted with worries that she might have saved Abel's life had she not left him to shield her son from Abel's latent violence. Hope begins a search to know the "true" Abel, a spy, and the book moves to Manila, Rome, Nashville and Washington, D. C.

The reader will see on the pages of any of Randall's novels the skill of an author who writes equally well about race, sex, violence, deceit, the intricacies of marriage and a number of other issues. Widely read and astute in her descriptions, Alice Randall takes the reader into multiple settings with finesse; her characters are as alive as the person standing in a room with the reader. She reveals the African American experience so that the reader cannot fail to understand the conflicting emotions within her central characters.

The first African American woman to write a number one country song, Alice Randall also wrote a video of the year, worked on multiple Johnny Cash videos and produced a pilot for a prime time drama on CBS (featuring ex-wives of country stars).

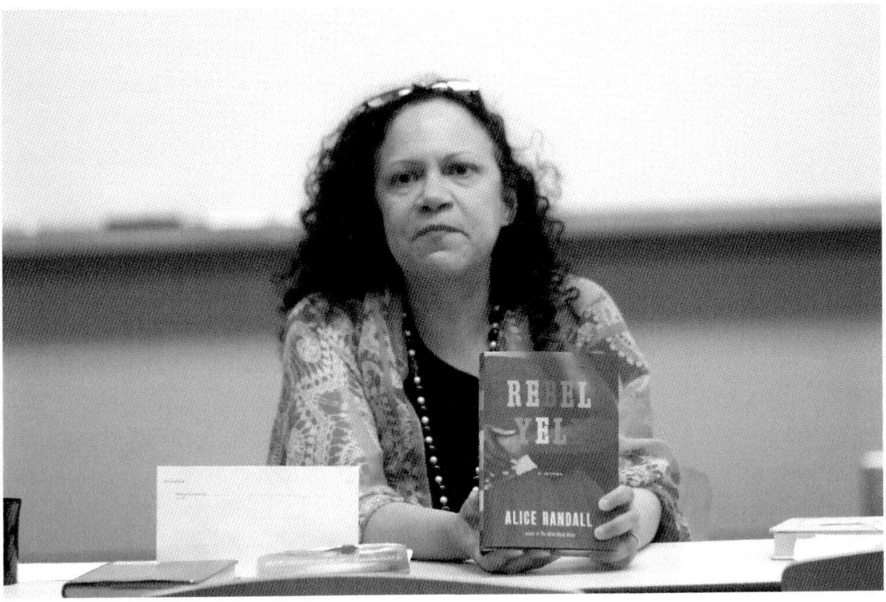


Alice Randall speaks to writers. *Bill Larson.*

Alice Randall discusses *Ada's Rules*. *Bill Larson.*

*Ada's Rules* hits head on what Alice Randall feels is the dominant civil rights issue of the first quarter of the twenty-first century: health disparity, specifically, the issue of being overweight that leads to diabetes in one in four African American women over fifty-five. Diabetes leads to many women suffering amputation or kidney failure. Alice Randall is on a crusade to help women recognize this problem and find ways to overcome it.

*Ada's Rules* is a novel that helps the reader learn about the life of Ada Howard, the wife of the pastor of Nashville's Full Love Gospel Tabernacle. Ada receives an invitation to her twenty-fifth class reunion and is then shocked to learn that she's eaten her way to 220 pounds. Deciding that she will lose 100 pounds in the next year, she writes a list of fifty-three rules, beginning with, "Don't keep doing what you've always been doing!"

Alice Randall is a master storyteller with myriad characters who surprise at every turn. Ada suspects that her husband, Lucius "Preach" Howard, has found a girlfriend. He's lost weight, cut his hair and has bought himself a new car. On top of that, he stays away from home quite a bit and says he needs to install a shower in his office. Preach and Ada have no sex life, and Ada sets out on a mission to correct that problem by "bringing her husband back to the table of her body."

## Well-Rounded Life

Alice Randall's background ranges from completing an independent study with Julia Child (and consequently teaching classes on soul food in addition to those on American culture and creative writing) to founding Midsummer Music to fund novel writing and a community of powerful storytellers in Nashville after her graduation from Harvard.

Most importantly, Alice Randall believes that motherhood is the most creative of callings. She is a sensitive, caring human being who devotes herself to lifting up the human race through philanthropy in many areas. With her attorney husband, David Ewing, she lives in Nashville but speaks throughout the United States. Their daughter, Caroline Williams, also a Harvard graduate, teaches and writes in the Mississippi Delta.

Her awards have been bestowed by such diverse groups as ASCAP (Silver Circle), Billboard Hot Country Singles Chart, Memphis Black Writers' Conference, Southern Film Festival, NAACP (Image Award) and the First Annual Mixed Media Watch Image Awards.

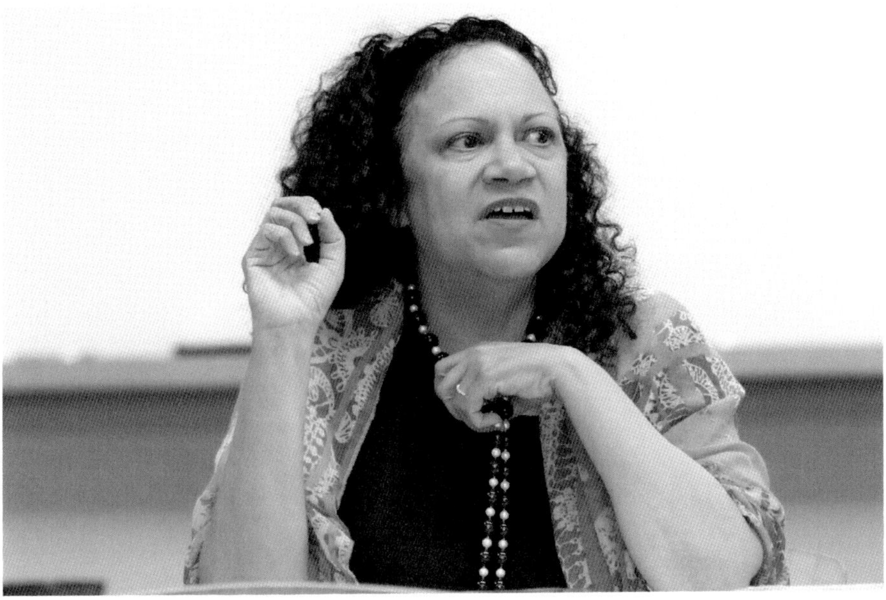

Alice Randall discusses her work at Clarksville Writers' Conference. *Bill Larson.*

## Home Life

Alice Randall, after graduation from Harvard, moved to Nashville when she was twenty-three. Her first husband, attorney Avon Williams III, proposed to her the day her first song, "Reckless Night," (described as a retelling of *The Scarlet Letter*) was recorded. They lived together for five years in places such as Martinique, the Philippines and Washington, D.C., but Alice says that her novel *Rebel Yell* is not autobiographical.

After her divorce from Williams, she moved back to Nashville with her three-year-old daughter. She founded Midsummer Music. With Matraca Berg, she wrote "Xxx's and Ooo's (An American Girl)," recorded by Trisha Yearwood. Of Alice's twenty songs that have been recorded, several have reached the top ten and top forty lists.

"I fell in love with country music as an art form," Alice relates. "I believe it to be the music of uneducated white people, and I want to stand up for their civil rights. I believe that Merle Haggard is one of our greatest American poets."

While at Harvard, in addition to her American literature studies major, Alice took an independent study in cooking with Julia Child. Alice began cooking when she was a child. She has a dining table that seats eighteen and likes to cook for large groups, even up to one hundred people at the time.

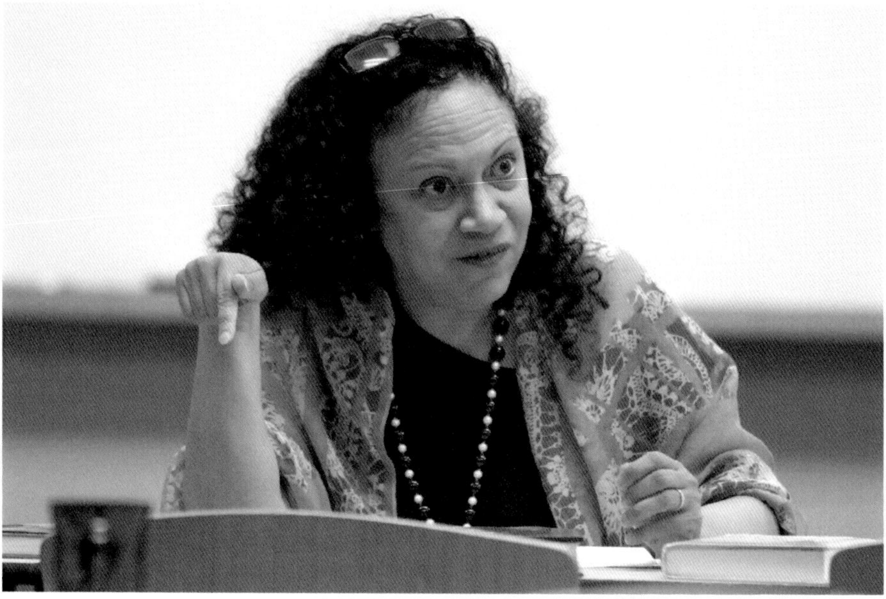

Making a point at Clarksville Writers' Conference, Alice Randall captivates the audience. *Bill Larson.*

Randall is now married to David Ewing, an attorney who practices green law. On the grounds of the Capitol during the inauguration of President Bill Clinton, Ewing (who is six feet, five inches tall) suddenly dropped to his knees in front of Alice.

"Being a neurotic worrier, I thought he had been shot or had a heart attack," she remembers. The crowd around them began applauding, and she realized that he was proposing.

Having formerly taught at Harvard, Princeton, the University of Virginia and Wesleyan, Alice Randall is now writer-in-residence at Vanderbilt University, where she teaches Country Lyric in American Culture, Creative Writing, and Soul Food. She contributes frequently to *Elle* magazine.

She has appeared on television scores of times and is quoted regularly in magazines and newspapers throughout the country. Coauthored with Carter and Courtney Little, her first book of nonfiction, *My Country Roots: The Ultimate MP3 Guide to America's Outsider Music*, has its introduction written by George Jones.

Even Starbucks loves Alice Randall. On their coffee cups, they have written her lines, "Mother-love is not inevitable. The good mother is a great artist ever creating beauty out of chaos." To date, more than five million of these cups have been distributed, and they continue to sell well.

## Social Media

Looking at Alice Randall's website is an adventure in itself. Numerous photographs link you to all types of information about Alice and her family. For instance, her daughter collects cookbooks, now housed in Alice's kitchen until her daughter moves into her own home.

Alice Randall was born in Detroit but grew up in Washington, D.C. During a lonely childhood, she discovered the library, where English detectives and the Brontë sisters captured her imagination. A political consultant, her mother (now deceased) divorced her father when Alice was in third grade. Alice felt that her mother, although glamorous, was "distant" and left her alone for long periods of time.

"I had to imagine my way into being a good mother," she said. "All parents don't love their children. There is no question in my mind that my mother did not love me. I certainly spent a lot of time loving her." Perhaps that's one reason Alice Randall describes motherhood as her most important occupation.

## Graceful Presence

It is impossible on a written page to describe the inner beauty of Alice Randall and her infinite kindness to others. Only those who have been in her presence and have been the object of her sympathetic words can begin to know the loving empathy she emits. Her active imagination extends to amazing depths on wide-ranging subjects that seem ever expanding—from food to health to racial equality to intense human interactions of every description.

Alice Randall is a frequent guest speaker at the Clarksville Writers' Conference at Austin Peay State University in Clarksville, Tennessee. Waiving all honorariums from the conference, she has served as its keynote speaker in addition to giving lectures on all her books for attendees.

Alice Randall has never acquired the self-importance and exalted self-worth that many famous writers seem to feel their due. Her demeanor is that of the woman next door. She shares her knowledge with college students on a weekly basis and opens her home and heart to others no matter their race, creed or intellectual persuasion.

Our society sometimes describes certain men as having the Renaissance state of mind of a Michelangelo or Leonardo, but it is in Alice Randall that a desire to reach the heights and depths of intellectual activity is located.

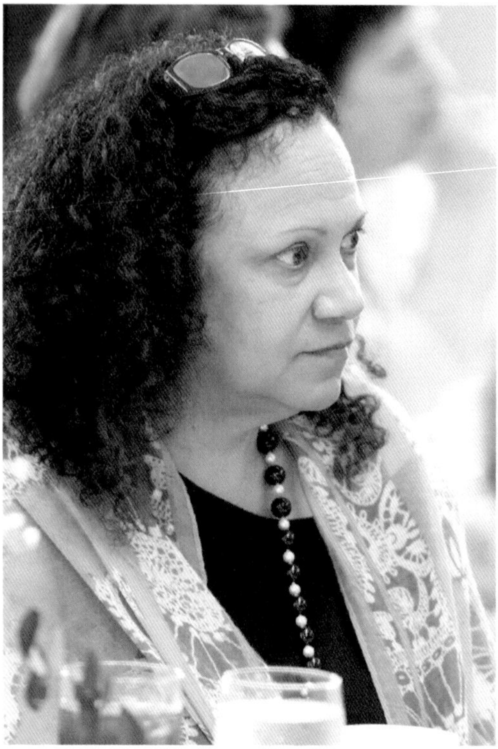

Alice Randall listens to questions. *Bill Larson.*

Here's a woman who can discuss Proust in one minute and serves cornbread madeleines to her guests. She has chairs in which Adam Clayton Powell, Malcolm X and Thurgood Marshall all sat, but she is friends with Lyle Lovett, George Jones and a host of country stars. She loves Nashville but writes to break down the barriers that have separated the races in the South for hundreds of years.

To read Alice Randall's books is to venture into a land where no holds are barred and to face your own worst prejudices head on.

John Seigenthaler, founder of the First Amendment Center and host of *A Word on Words* seen on PBS, says about her, "Alice Randall has given us Hope [referring to the character in *Rebel Yell*]. And Hope helps us understand that black and white, more than a definition of contrasting colors and more than a means of identifying two races, is the sum of our dark past, our glowing present and our bright future."

CHAPTER EIGHT

# AMY GREENE

## *APPALACHIAN NOVELIST*

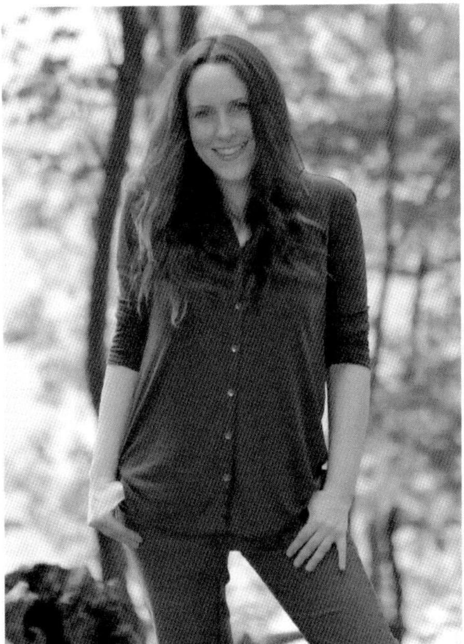

Amy Greene. *Photography by Adam Greene.*

Amy Greene has done something that few writers can boast. Her first novel was snapped up by Alfred A. Knopf, a major publishing company, within one week of its being offered by her agent. The chance of this happening is so minute, it doesn't even bear calculating. She hadn't even sold a short story prior to that.

*Bloodroot*, Amy's novel about a mother and her twins who live in Appalachia, was read by Jill McCorkle (author of five books on the *New York Times* Notable Books list) at the 2007 Sewanee Writers' Conference. McCorkle was so impressed that she offered to put Amy in touch with agent Leigh Feldman when the book was finished.

Amy quickly finished *Bloodroot* and was consequently in contact with Ms. Feldman, who sent the manuscript to ten different publishers. Immediately

Alfred A. Knopf—within the first week—responded that they were purchasing the book for publication.

Every year on or near her birthday, Amy Greene visits Dollywood, the theme park located in East Tennessee near where Amy, her husband and two children live. "When I was a little girl, it was called Silver Dollar City. It was a great joy of my life. There were no vacations. My parents worked all the time," Amy explains. It was while she was in Dollywood that she received a call from Leigh Feldman who told Amy that she would like to represent her as her agent. Amy said she was trying to conceal the fact that she was at Dollywood but when the train went by, she could no longer hide the fact.

Later on, when Amy had her daughter, who was ill, at the pediatrician's office, she received another phone call from Leigh Feldman. Feldman had warned Greene that if she received a call from her early on, it would most likely be a rejection. Amy revealed, "She said we had an offer, a preemptive offer, which means they wanted us to rescind offering it to the other publishers! It was the best ever!"

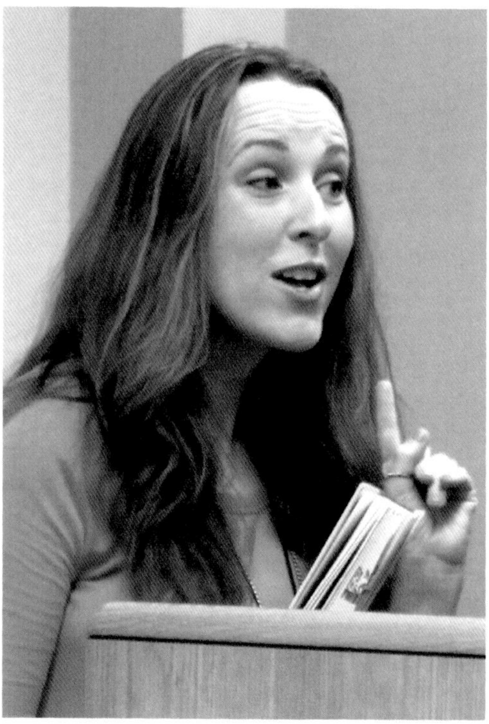

Amy Greene reading from *Bloodroot*. *Sue Freeman Culverhouse*.

To state that this was a once-in-a-million happening is to understate the situation. Many authors have been rejected scores of times before they are accepted, and Amy was truly being published for the first time ever.

The rest is history. *Bloodroot* was on the "extended" *New York Times* bestseller list and on the American Library Association list. The *Entertainment Weekly* review gave it an *A*, and it was on the publication's "must" list. Amy admits that this was one of those moments when she realized what was happening. "I was in the moment, and the thing that I had wanted to do since I was a child had happened," Amy said in a phone interview on January 25, 2013.

## THE RESULTS OF PUBLICATION

For the next two years, Amy was involved in an extensive book tour and gave speeches all over the country. The magical aspect of her book brought scores of questions from professional interviewers and readers alike. Amy explains how magic was part of her life growing up:

> *Magic and haints* [ghosts] *were the background of my life. Once my mom got a phone call from one of her friends in Dyer Holler down the road from us. Dyer Holler was where we'd drive to see foxfire in the woods. Mom's friend said, "We're having to move out of our house because it's hainted." She was dead serious. I was a little girl but the best I remember was that the haint was throwing things around like a poltergeist. If you think about it, the mountain people are very practical people. Yet it is interesting that this dynamic of magic is alongside this practicality. It came across the ocean with the first settlers. One of the elements of living here is the hard life beside the beauty and magic. It makes a complicated place but that makes a wonderful place about which to write.*

One of the hardest parts of writing *Bloodroot* was putting all the voices together and making a cohesive story. "I was inspired by reading *All the Pretty Horses*, where the characters speak as I speak," she said. Amy loves books about Appalachian culture, and they helped her realize that the problems of people there are universal ones.

Amy drew from the admonitions of folklore from her childhood in writing the book. She had been told, for instance, never to pick up a bag beside the road because it might have somebody's warts in it. She weaves a "cure" for thrush (called "thresh" in the mountains) masterfully into the plot of *Bloodroot.* (Thrush is a yeast infection of the mucus membrane lining of the mouth and tongue.) Byrdie has her mouth breathed into by a "man who didn't know his daddy" (the criteria necessary to cure thrush according to mountain lore). Byrdie goes to the home of a man named Clifford, and "he blowed warm wind in my mouth and down my swelled-up throat." Both Byrdie and her grandmother "felt the power."

Authors always have mixed feelings about the publication of their work. Greene recalled, "I think before the book was published, I was afraid of a negative reaction or that it would be ignored. *Bloodroot* is not unicorns and rainbows. The book is about magic, but it's not always pretty. I worried about the perception of my family and friends. I had underestimated

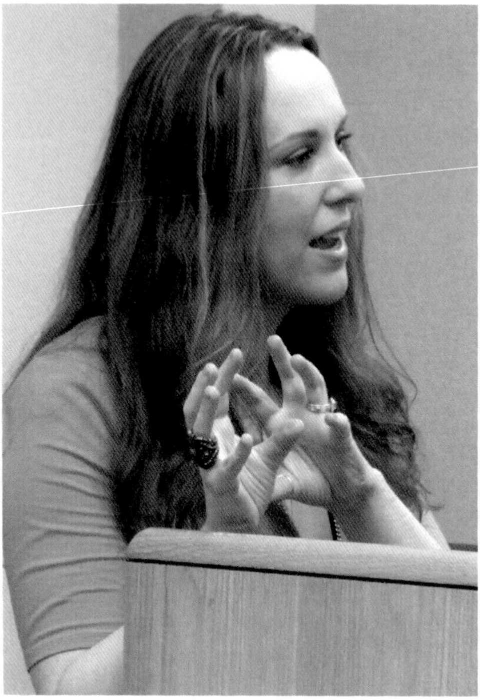

the joy and kindness from my community. The newspaper, the local community college and my hometown have been so supportive. My family—even my Uncle Junior!—read it. They read it because they love me. Because I put so much of my real self in the book, I think they took their perceptions of me aside and enjoyed the book."

Amy Greene talks to other writers. *Sue Freeman Culverhouse.*

## SECOND NOVEL

*Long Man*, taking its title from the name the Cherokee called the Tennessee River, is about a little girl who became lost about a month before her town is to be flooded by a dam required by the Tennessee Valley Authority.

Amy Greene admits that TVA has been good for East Tennessee because in her own family, her grandfather was a subsistence farmer. The advent of TVA allowed her parents to go to work in a factory and have more economic advantages. However, when summer now lowers the level of Cherokee Lake near Amy's home, she can see the tops of silos and the former roads that led to the area that was flooded. She thinks of the homes that used to be and the people who lived there. The tantalizing imaginations of her fertile mind are making her new novel one that is eagerly awaited.

She recalled that writing *Long Man* was a completely different experience from writing her first book. She explains that *Bloodroot* was character driven. "I had the idea first for *Long Man.* I started to write a linear novel, but when I got about a third of the way through, I didn't know the characters enough. I went back and did the character studies like I did in *Bloodroot.*"

In the meantime, she's hard at work on her third novel. At least for 2013, she has turned down all speaking engagements to concentrate on her family and writing her next book. She writes sitting up in bed with pencil and paper in hand just as she always has.

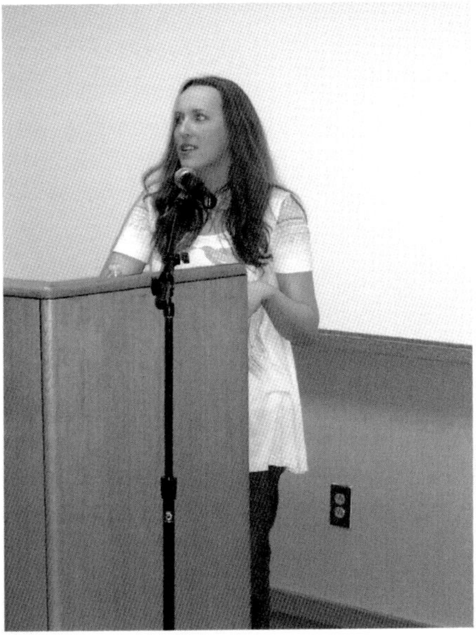

Amy Greene answers audience questions. *Sue Freeman Culverhouse.*

Success has made few outward changes in Amy's life. "What is really interesting is that I live in the same house ten minutes down the road from my parents. The success of my book just made things easier. I can write full time. I don't have to worry as much about money as I used to. The pressure is off for now. I'm just living my life, and I don't think about it often. I bought my husband a Jeep. We always had to worry about cars breaking down before," Amy said.

She continued:

> *I thought that if you made it into the* New York Times, *you'd be filthy rich, but that's not the way it works. I think I'm making about a dollar a copy off my paperback. The advance helps you to finish the book. You don't get rich unless Oprah touches you with her magic wand. I got lucky because most writers still are working at a college or can't support themselves from the proceeds of the book. I got really lucky. My experience is not typical. If my next novel doesn't do well, I* [might] *be working at Sonic or something.* Bloodroot *bought me a few years of stability.*

## PERSONAL LIFE

Amy Greene gives her parents a great deal of credit for supporting her dreams. "Although my dad worked in a factory and my mom cleaned houses and worked in tobacco, they never told me I couldn't be a writer. My father was a wonderful painter but he would never have thought of going to art school because he was told that he couldn't support a family by being an artist."

Her family is always at the center of her life. Her husband, Adam, and she met when they were teenagers. Adam has always been extremely supportive of Amy's writing:

> *Adam is a freelance sports writer and sports photographer. He takes mostly photos of baseball or basketball—and I'm his side job. He freelances for several different newspapers, and he works for Carson-Newman College. Somehow, we made the right decision for ourselves. He was two years into college. When I was right out of high school, we decided to get married. (My parents did the same thing when they decided to get married right out of school.) They were happy because they love Adam too. They were supportive of us. By the time I was twenty, I had my son. It was unexpected. I wanted to write. I spent the time as a young mother just reading and writing. In the daytime, I was reading. When Adam got home from working construction, he would take over so I could go into my room and write. He's always been a huge supporter. We have always been partners.*

Greene also spoke of her children:

> *My son, Taylor, is seventeen and my daughter, Emma, is ten. We are a really close family who share hugs every day. Emma has posters from my book tour in her room, but neither of my kids wants to go to any of my speeches. Taylor loves video games and fantasy, but one day he said, "Mom, I've got to get better reading material. After all, I'm the son of Amy Greene!"*

## Outreach

Amy Greene loves to share her experience with other aspiring writers. First, she admits an undying admiration for Dolly Parton, another Appalachian woman who has found herself on the world stage:

> *I love Dolly! She's my role model in a way. She is herself all the time. She's not ashamed of her roots.*
>
> *When I was in New York for the first time, I was reading at a library. Two other people—one from Columbia University—were reading too. I was completely different from them. I thought of Dolly. She's the same*

*person all the time. I decided that I was just going to be me. It worked! A lot of people crowded around me and wanted to talk to me. I didn't try to change and be someone else. I go to Dollywood every year because I love Dolly and because one of the best moments of my life happened there, so why not!*

Winner of the Tennessee Writer of the Year from the Tennessee Writer's Alliance and the Weatherford Award for Fiction from Berea College, Amy Greene has been a reader all her life, and it is from this fact that she admonishes all writers to read constantly. "The truest thing I can tell anyone who wants to write is to read constantly. Devour books. You never stop learning. If you ever get complacent, you're not going to grow. Reading and writing are totally intertwined."

Since her childhood, when her mother and she would go to the public library in Morristown, Tennessee, to check out books, Amy has read constantly. "I couldn't afford to buy books then, but I never stopped reading," she recalled. "I also read voraciously when I was a young mother. That's when I was setting the stage for my writing career."

Another piece of advice she has is to write consistently. "I had to learn to trust myself. I abandoned tons of novels when I was in my twenties. I would let it go. I learned that I couldn't take more than three days off! If I did, I might lose it. Now I trust myself and believe I'll pick it up, but then, I had to learn to set limits for myself. You can lose your entire novel if you don't keep working," she insists.

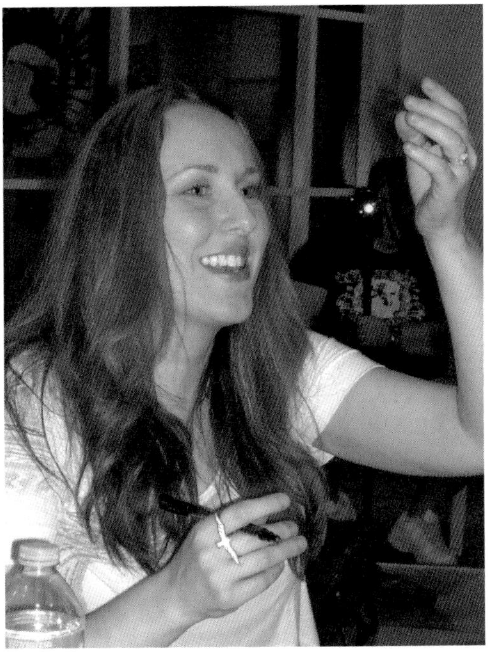

Amy Greene at book signing at Austin Peay State University. *Sue Freeman Culverhouse.*

"You have to examine your heart. You have to figure out your motive for writing. If you would write if you were on a deserted island, you should be a writer. If you have any other motivation, you should do something else. I spend many times fourteen hours in a day writing. It's hard, but it's necessary. It feels good to me in the end," she continued.

"I think Stephen King said, 'Unless you're obsessed with this, you will never be great.' The reason I'm still a writer is because I don't really care if my editor doesn't like this. I want to write it, and it has nothing to do with publishing. I'm writing for me. Writing has to be its own reward."

Amy Greene is grounded in three pleasures. She insists, "My joys are my family, reading and writing. They are essential to my happiness."

CHAPTER NINE

# A. SCOTT PEARSON

## *NOVELIST, CANCER RESEARCHER, SURGEON AND PATIENT ADVOCATE*

Born in Brownsville, Tennessee, A. Scott Pearson is the son of Wilder and Norma Pearson. His father lived on and farmed the same land all his life. His mother taught elementary school for some fifty years.

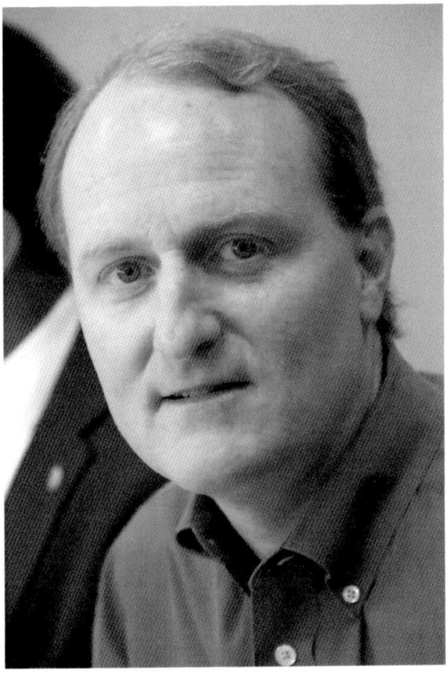

Dr. A. Scott Pearson. *Bill Larson.*

In a scripted interview, Scott recalled, "We lived eighteen miles from town. When I was five, my parents decided it was too much trouble to get me to kindergarten. So, I stayed home with my grandmother who read *Treasure Island* out loud to me and convinced me that my great-great-great grandfather was a pirate. I still like to believe that. Sitting at my father's oak desk, on his Remington typewriter, I typed the opening chapters of Robert Louis Stevenson's classic. Perhaps the year I skipped kindergarten was a foreshadowing."

He attended Tennessee Academy in Brownsville, a small school where he graduated with twenty-three fellow classmates. The school closed its doors two years later.

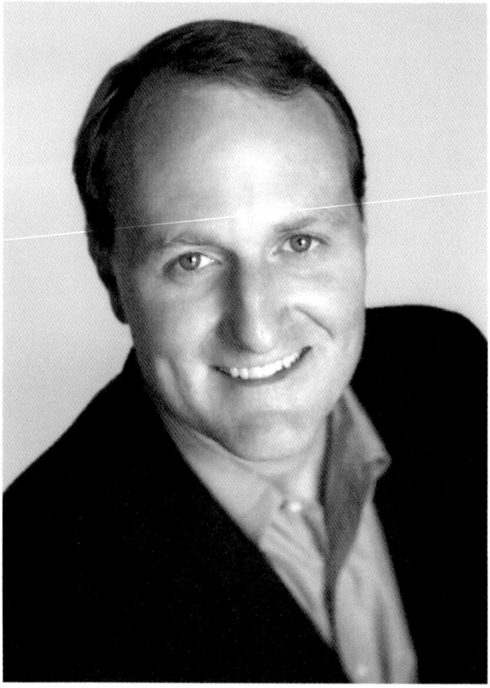

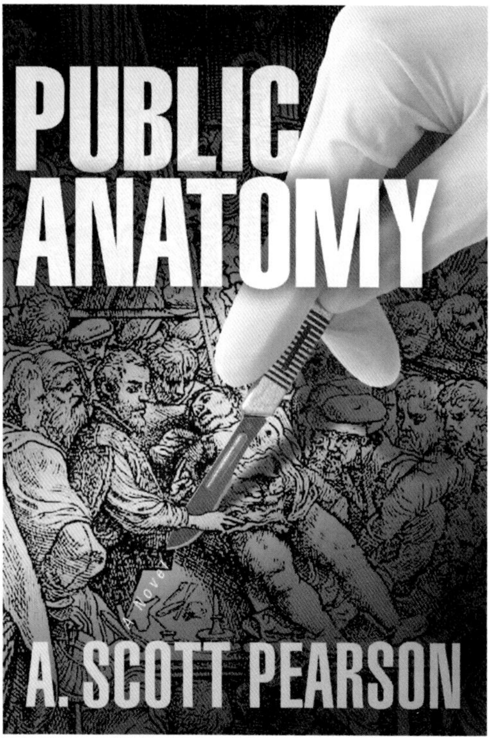


Scott admits that his grandmothers had great influence on his life. "Both of my grandmothers were strong-willed, hardworking women with a great sense of faith and family," he told me.

As for becoming a doctor, he said that he had "no immediate doctors in the family except for my great-grandfather who was a family physician (and grandson of the pirate, I suppose). A traumatic event led me toward medicine. When I was fifteen, while painting our house in the summer, my father ran into the blade of a backhoe, which peeled back his scalp. In the rear of our station wagon, I held pressure with a blood-soaked towel while my mother drove the twenty miles to the hospital. He had quite a scar to show for that."

Tennessee has been Dr. Pearson's home for most of his life: "I have lived all over the state of Tennessee. I was born in Brownsville, Tennessee (seat of Haywood County), and raised in the rich upper-

*Top*: Dr. A. Scott Pearson, cancer specialist and author of *Rupture* and *Public Anatomy*. *Courtesy of A. Scott Pearson.*

*Bottom*: *Public Anatomy* by A. Scott Pearson.

delta land of the Forked Deer farming community. I was in Knoxville for college at the University of Tennessee and in Memphis for medical school at the University of Tennessee. After eight years of surgical training in Texas, I moved back to Tennessee, and my current home in Nashville." His wife, Robin, is from Chattanooga, and they visit there often. They met in Memphis while Scott was in medical school and married during his fourth year just before moving to Texas.

## Birth of Eli Branch

Dr. A. Scott Pearson debuted his first book, *Rupture*, in 2010. On June 4, 2012, Dr. Pearson's Benjamin Franklin Award for Mysteries was announced by the Independent Book Publishers Association at a ceremony at the Marriott Marquis Hotel in New York. This was awarded for his second novel, *Public Anatomy*, introduced in March 2011. The Independent Book Publishers Association (IBPA) is the largest nonprofit association representing independent book publishers.

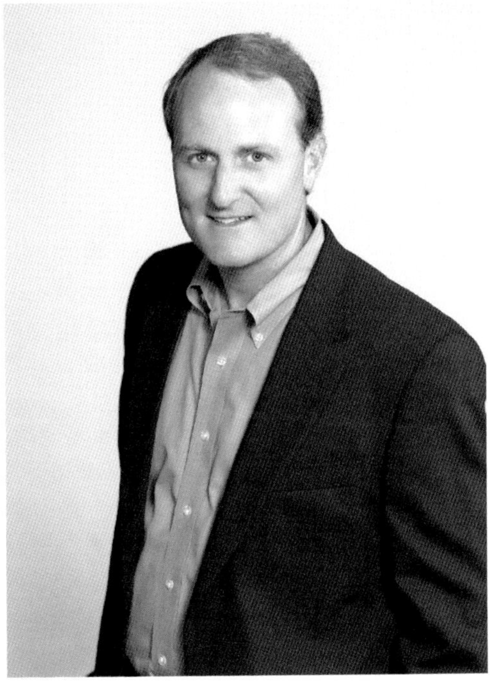

A. Scott Pearson, winner of the Benjamin Franklin Award for Mysteries from the Independent Book Publishers Association. *Courtesy of A. Scott Pearson.*

"My publisher notified me that I was one of three authors nominated," Scott wrote. "I was both surprised and delighted to win, but I was not able to attend the award ceremony in New York."

His many fans will be delighted to know that he is working on another novel. "I'm in the midst of book three featuring surgeon Eli Branch. This book is more of an international suspense thriller and takes place in Europe in addition to Memphis," he revealed.

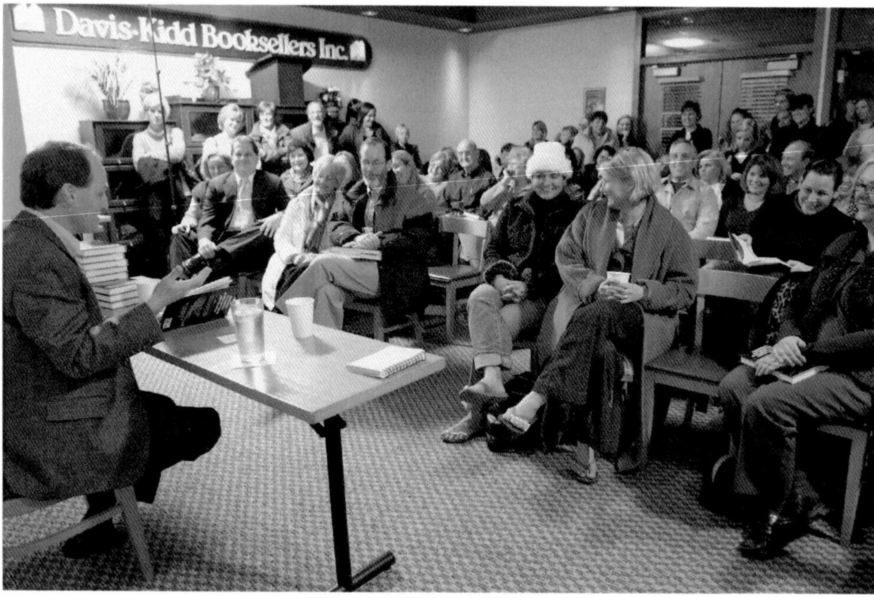


A. Scott Pearson at Davis-Kidd book signing. *Courtesy of A. Scott Pearson.*

Numerous book signings are part of every writer's life. "Being a surgeon-author makes for interesting interactions at book signings. I once had a reader pull down their pants to show me a surgical scar," Scott remembered with his wry sense of humor. "As I recall, the line got much shorter after that."

Surprisingly, when asked if most of his students know of his novels, he said, "Not as many students are aware as you might think. But I show them I'm an author by asking questions during my lectures and giving away a book to the student with the answers."

*Public Anatomy* again features Eli Branch, the physician who had his debut in *Rupture*. Branch encounters Dr. Liza French, a colleague he hasn't seen in ten years. Liza uses their past to entice Eli into her turbulent world in which her career is in jeopardy at a Memphis hospital.

A forensic pathologist, Dr. Meg Daily, who was also featured in *Rupture*, aids Eli in uncovering a pattern to the escalating deaths, and the search begins for the killer who the media and the city come to know as the Organist. Clues lead Eli to a sixteenth-century manuscript by an anatomist whose methods of dissection are over four centuries old but are being reenacted in the present.

Although the novel can be read without prior knowledge of the characters, *Public Anatomy* is best read after *Rupture*. A fellow novelist has asserted that Dr. Pearson is to medical mysteries what John Grisham is to legal ones.

## PATIENT ADVOCATE

A surgeon on the faculty and staff at Vanderbilt in Nashville, Dr. Pearson was also a member of the Interdisciplinary Group at the Robert Penn Warren Center for Humanities. Dr. Pearson teaches a class entitled "Narrative Medicine: Stories of Illness and the Doctor-Patient Relationship" to introduce premedical students to this patient-centered concept when they enter the fast-paced, technological race that defines today's medicine.

Dr. Pearson is passionate not only about writing novels but also about the need for teaching prehealth undergraduates and medical students to listen to the patient. In spite of all the new technology in medicine, he teaches that the patient's story is still essential in healing.

"The students are intrigued to learn that I believe the patient's narrative is as important as the biomedical data," Dr. Pearson reported. "In general, patients want their providers to know more about them in the context of their illness. We physicians could do a much better job with this."

## VIEWS ON WRITING

Dr. Pearson reminds readers that physicians write constantly: progress notes, clinic notes, notes to referring physicians, e-mails, letters to insurance companies, etc. Literature has a long history of physicians who also wrote novels—Robin Cook, Michael Crichton, Michael Palmer and many others.

He quotes W. Somerset Maugham as saying that there are three rules for writing a novel, but unfortunately, no one knows what they are.

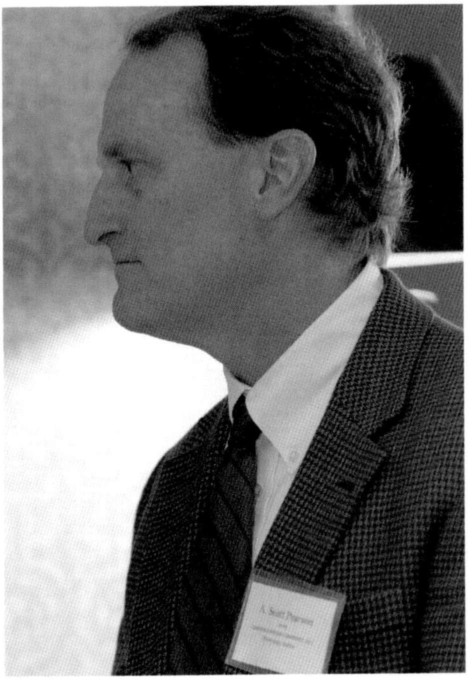

Dr. Pearson listens to audience questions. *Bill Larson.*

Dr. Pearson says that the three phases for writing a novel for him were: (1) the solitary, boring part of the actual writing; (2) publishing—and he asserts that getting into medical school was easier than this phase; and (3) the promotion and marketing when he actually gets to speak with his readers.

"Readers can truly read your book so closely that they can find any error you have made," he said. One reader pointed out that in *Rupture*, Dr. Pearson said that a Honda Civic "fishtailed," but "Civics can't fishtail because they have front wheel drive," the reader chided.

Dr. Pearson's character Eli Branch works in Memphis because Dr. Pearson himself went to medical school at the University of Tennessee there and is familiar with the setting on a first-person basis.

He reveals that one of his greatest moments came on March 8, 2011, after a book signing at Davis-Kidd (a famous bookstore in Nashville that has now gone out of business), when he was told that *Rupture* was number one on the fiction bestseller list with John Grisham's most recent book as number two.

Dr. Pearson said that the night before he was to appear on the televised book show *A Word on Words* on PBS, he was reading through his books again. His wife asked him why he was doing that. Dr. Pearson said that John Siegenthaler asks the most detailed questions about every aspect of the book—and never uses any notes. Dr. Pearson wanted to be sure that he could give the answers equally as well.

The picture on the front of *Public Anatomy* shows a plate from *De Humani Corporis Fabrica Libri Septum (On the Structure of the Human Body)*, published in 1555 and written by Andreas Vesalius, a surgeon to kings of Spain and France. Prior to this time, knowledge of the human body was based on dissections of dogs and monkeys since it was forbidden in those times to dissect a human being. The picture shows the public dissection of a female who had been hanged. She had claimed that she was pregnant, and because Vesalius insisted that only by dissecting a human being could accurate information be gained, he was allowed to dissect this woman. The only human dissections at that time were of criminals recently removed from the gallows. Anyone could view these dissections, which were held in the open on a stage constructed with bleachers to accommodate the crowds.

A page from this book is featured in *Public Anatomy* when it is discovered next to a murder victim. Eli Branch is called to the scene of the murder to assist police when this is discovered.

Dr. Pearson somehow fits writing novels into his otherwise amazingly busy life. His wife and he have two sons, and he's actively involved in their lives on a daily basis.

His writing schedule involves working at least forty-five minutes every morning (very early every morning, he admits) about five days a week. He follows the premise that if you write a page a day, at the end of a year, you have a book-length manuscript completed—or nearly completed.

"I started writing in an attempt to understand some events in my medical life," he told his readers. *Rupture* is actually the second book he's written. His first manuscript, set in 1970, is about a thirteen-year-old boy who is caretaker for an African American woman who can't receive the care she needs otherwise. It's still for sale.

"I met the publisher of *Rupture* at a writers' conference in 2007," he reports. "Now I have an agent, but then I didn't."

Perhaps Dr. Pearson's attitude toward patients is what led to his interest in writing medical novels. He quotes Hippocrates: "It is more important to know what person the disease has than to know what disease the person has." In other words, Dr. Pearson is interested in the person's life before, during and after the illness.

"We teach students about the disease and how to treat it in med school," he said, "but it's harder to teach them this softer side." Howard Winn (who had been a patient of Dr. Pearson at Vanderbilt) interjected during Dr. Pearson's speech at the writers' conference in Clarksville that the first time he met Dr. Pearson, he was struck by the amount of time Scott spent getting to know him as a person and in understanding his life and work.

## NARRATIVE MEDICINE

Dr. Pearson truly believes that narrative medicine—learning the patient's story—is critical in optimizing healthcare. He said that the push in medicine to see more patients in a shorter time in order to make more money for hospitals (and physicians themselves) is a great challenge today.

Scott feels that the socioeconomic conditions in which a patient lives, the geographic location of the patient's home and whatever is specific to that patient is the basis for narrative-based medicine. As a result, he teaches a class in narrative medicine for undergraduate students who believe they want to go into the medical field of study.

He actually asks these students to keep journals about their experiences with illness. "The class is fun to teach and is enjoyable for students," he insists.

"We surgeons alter the quality of life and intervene at a very invasive level, especially for cancer patients," he explained. "I've actually operated on one patient twelve times. We have to think more broadly about patient care."

## Why He Writes

*Rupture* followed Dr. Pearson's research into the approach of other medical writers. "I slept through most of high school English classes," he admits, "so I had some work to do."

"I'm constantly revising," Scott said, "but I finally end up with a completed manuscript. In my early writing years, I was very naïve and had no contacts in publishing at all. I experienced the eighty-first rejection as I learned that selling a book is a whole art in itself."

He went on: "It took me about eighteen months from the signed contract through the editing era that involved checking facts and dates, and then the press reviews were next. About six months before *Rupture* came out, I decided to look it up on Google. I found it on a site that dealt with hemorrhoids and, later, on a Scandinavian tummy tuck site!" It is obvious that Dr. Pearson not only has a sense of humor but is also not overly impressed with his own accomplishments.

The medical thriller *Rupture* takes place in Memphis at the "University of Mid-south Medical College." Eli Branch, a young surgeon-scientist and the son of a renowned professor of anatomy at this same school, discovers the dark side of medicine and a web of lies as more and more victims meet sudden and violent deaths. He links up with Meg Daily, a forensic pathologist, in a life-and-death race against time.

The title of the book reveals Scott's metaphor for the disruption between medicine and the trust of society. The book is a definite page-turner.

Scott Pearson is not of the "I'm the exalted doctor; you are the lowly patient" school of medicine. He is anything but a man impressed with himself. Personable, easy to talk to, open about his opinions but not willing to force them on anyone else, Dr. Pearson is a typical "guy next door" who is out to make a difference in this world. The underlying messages in his books reveal a reality check on modern medicine—its advances and its failures. He graphically points out potential societal grief that can result from the cramming of too many patients into too little time and the behind-the-scenes politics that rule the hospitals of today.

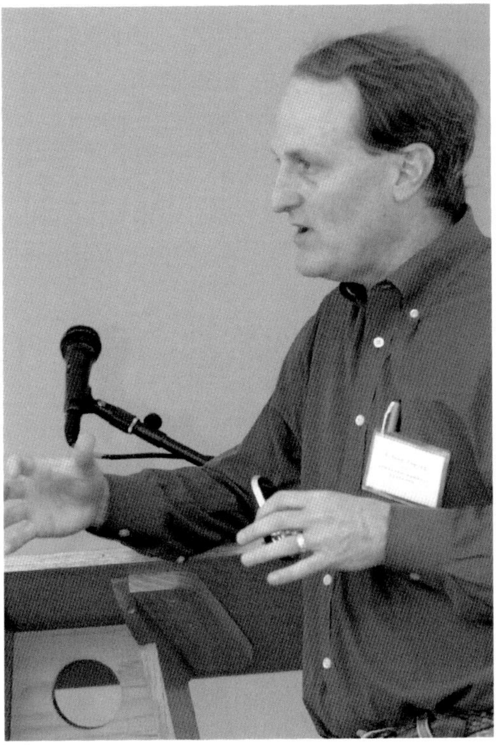

Scott Pearson speaks to other writers. *Bill Larson.*

His open and smiling demeanor rewards readers with whom he comes into contact. Another reward is the opportunity to quiz him on not only his books but also his feelings about how the future of medicine needs to focus not on the mercenary aspects of the field but on a patient care based on the life of the patient. Dr. Pearson writes a blog on his website that reveals even more about his character. Called Pens and Scalpels, the blog describes patients who have come to him because of cancer or because of unknown illnesses. A touching episode about a tobacco farmer who gave him some leaves of the plant as a memento is not to be missed nor is the comedic description of his mother's fire-wielding approach to ticks.

Pearson's life as a writer has had its own advantages. "I've enjoyed interacting with fellow physician-author Abraham Verghese, who is multitalented in both fiction and nonfiction," he said. "I've met Robin Cook, who I consider the creator of the medical thriller genre, and Stephen King, who has quite a following!"

If Dr. Pearson's name is not yet a household word, don't let that fool you. His series about Eli Branch is coming into the public consciousness one book at a time. He admitted that if "at some point in the future the opportunity arises, I would consider writing full time."

Dr. Pearson's advice to aspiring writers is, "Everyone is busy. Most people don't have four or five hours a day to write. Leave something off. Don't wait until you have days or weeks in a row to write…Take what time you have."

CHAPTER TEN

# MARSHALL CHAPMAN

*AUTHOR, ROCKER, SONGWRITER, ACTRESS EXTRAORDINAIRE*

Born in Spartanburg, South Carolina, on January 7, 1949, Martha Marshall Chapman II is the daughter of a cotton millowner and grew up in a somewhat privileged environment. Although her family had plans for her life as a debutante, Marshall went to an Elvis Presley concert in 1957 and began her life as a totally free spirit from that moment on.

At six feet tall, Marshall is uninhibited and original in thought, word and deed. She's been described as "a force of nature" by author Peter Gurainick, but no four words can ever tell you what a presence you find yourself in when you're in the room with Marshall. You just never know what's going to happen next.

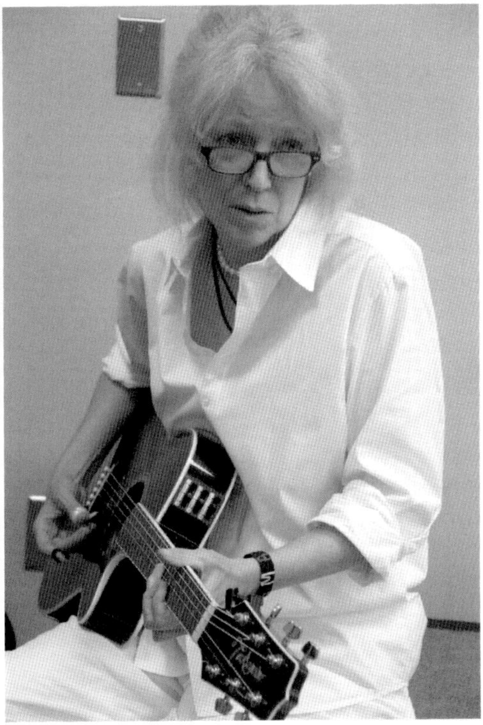

Marshall Chapman. *Bill Larson.*

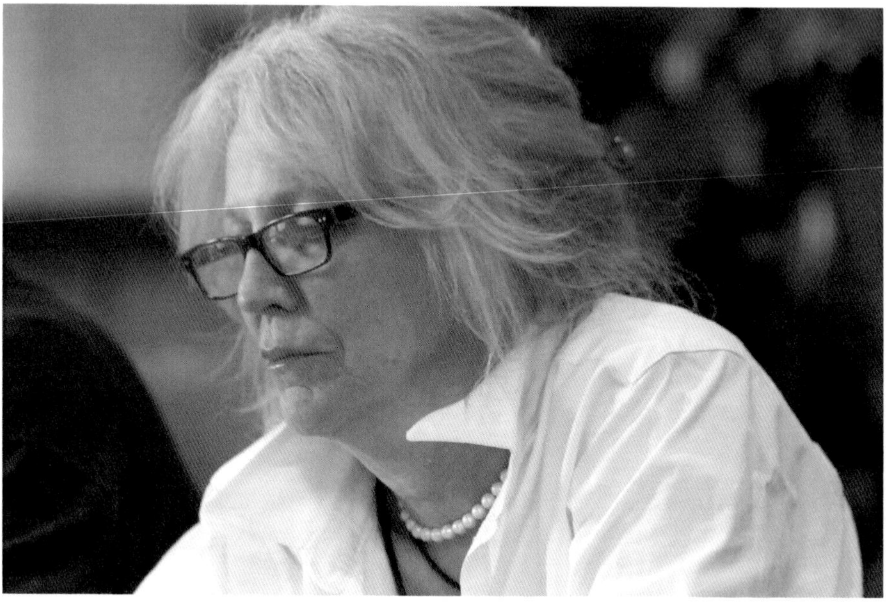

Marshall Chapman edits a manuscript. *Bill Larson.*

## INTO HER MIND

Her autobiography, *Goodbye, Little Rock-and-Roller*, features a front cover with Marshall in the nude on her lounge chair giving someone (the photographer? the reader? the world?) a universal symbol with her third finger. The stories in the book will make you laugh until tears run down your face—and alternately cry at the depth of her anguish. Her description of the scene at her parents' home when her only brother died is totally unforgettable. No one could make this up.

*Goodbye, Little Rock-and-Roller* was a finalist for Southern Independent Booksellers Association Nonfiction Book of the Year.

> *Patience was never one of my virtues. It was something I had to pray about, as in "Oh Lord, grant me patience...and grant it to me now!"*
>
> *Marshall Chapman,* Goodbye, Little Rock and Roller

Marshall went to see Elvis with her family's six-foot-tall maid, Cora Jeter. Cora sat in the front of the bus with Marshall beside her in spite of the stares of the bus driver because she told the man, "Drive your bus, man. My feets is tired." (Cora did have bad feet and wore men's wingtip shoes with stragetic holes for toes and bunions, according to Marshall.) When they reached the

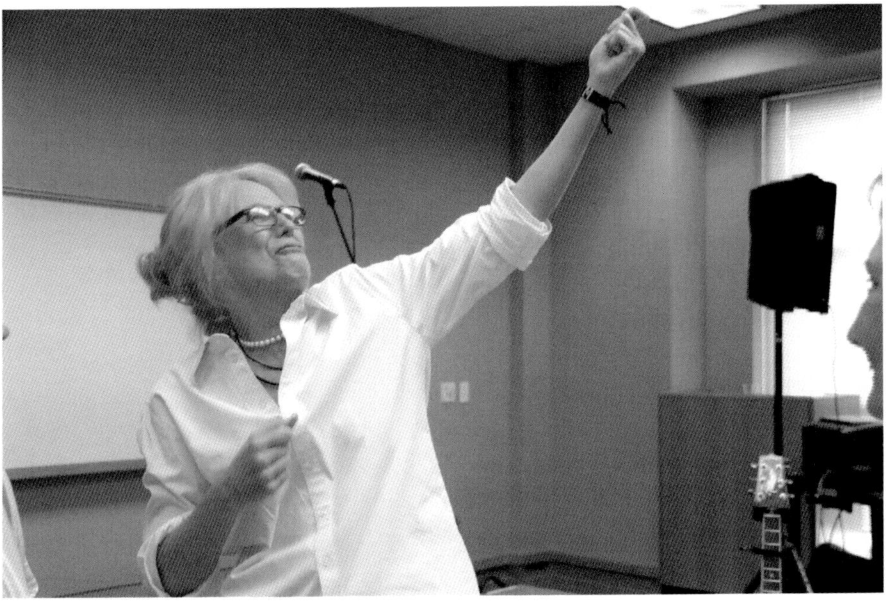

Marshall Chapman in a blaze of glory. *Bill Larson.*

Carolina Theater, Cora and seven-year-old Marshall sat in the "colored balcony" because every other seat was sold out. Marshall also remembers that Justin Tubb, the Louvin Brothers, the Carter Sisters and Benny Martin were performing that day. After the around thirty minutes that Elvis was on stage, life had a totally new meaning for Marshall. Something in her soul was bonded forever, and she never looked back.

Seven-year-old Marshall wrote a letter to Elvis with only the address, "Hollywood, Calif." on it. Although her mother figured she was sending her letter off into the dead letter office, Marshall received a manila folder with two "signed" Elvis photographs and an Elvis catalog. Marshall, with her mother's help, ordered an Elvis T-shirt and sailor's cap, which she then wore to school daily—and even slept in the shirt. (Her mother would have to bribe her to take it off long enough for it to be washed.)

## FORGET BEING A DEBUTANTE

After her graduation from a boarding school—Salem Academy in Winston-Salem, North Carolina—Chapman went to Vanderbilt University in 1967.

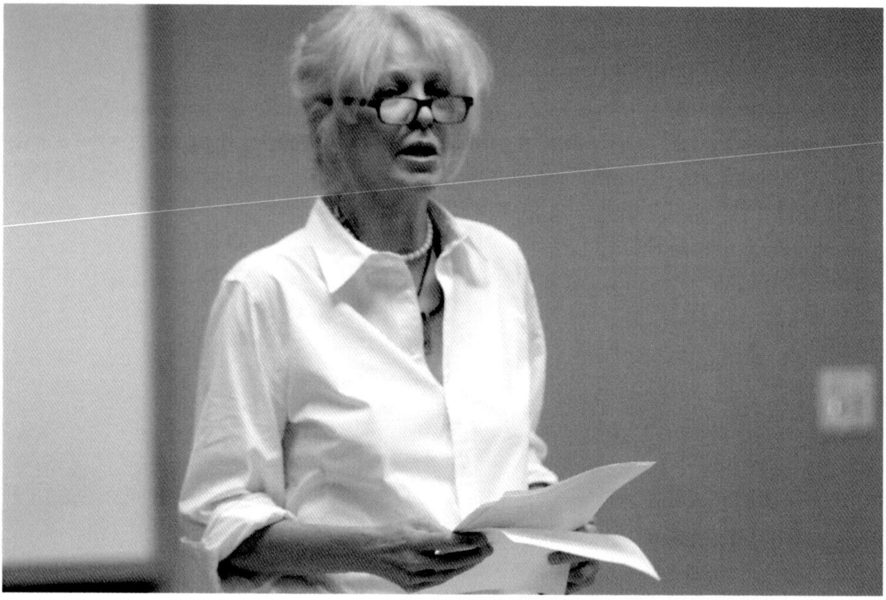

Marshall Chapman talks about her friend William Gay. *Bill Larson.*

She spent one summer touring Europe and her junior year staying in Aix-en-Provence. She told Charlotte J. Robertson in an interview, "Straight from a Woman's Heart," that she hitchhiked to Crete in 1969 and lived in a Monoan cave with some hippies near Matala. Then, during her senior year at Vanderbilt, she commuted to Nashville from New York, where she spent most of her time with her new love; she basically showed up for midterms and exams. She claims that her French major was designed so that she'd have to become a musician since she would not be prepared for a regular job. (Never underestimate the intelligence of this woman nor her ability to surprise you at every turn.)

> *I believe there is a connection between not looking for love and finding it…*
> *But first, I had to give up my career of dating criminals.*
> *Marshall Chapman,* Goodbye, Little Rock-and-Roller

After her graduation from Vanderbilt, Marshall spent the next few years playing in small clubs in Nashville, where she earned a reputation as being the "wildest female rock-n-roll bandleader" with her band, Jaded Virgin.

## Songwriter for the Stars

One night when her friend Danny Flowers (writer of "Tulsa Time," a multigenre hit) was playing guitar for Marshall, he told her that if she didn't start writing songs, she'd never get out of the "joints" and make it big. She went home that night and wrote her first song, "A Woman's Heart (Is a Handy Place to Be)." It was later recorded by Crystal Gayle on her first album and also recorded by country singer Jessi Colter on her second album.

Later in 1973, Marshall spent time in London with her friend artist Stone Roberts. Several other Vanderbilt women were on the scene, and Marshall's best friend, Helen Bransford, was seeing Isaac Tigret, who had just opened the Hard Rock Cafe near Picadilly Circus.

In the fall of 1974, Marshall toured New Zealand and Australia with the Roger Miller Show. Her first trip west of the Mississippi and her first road trip with a band were thrilling experiences for Marshall.

When she returned to the States, she stayed in Los Angeles for a couple of weeks and went to hear Willie Nelson one night at the Troubadour. Marshall considers hearing Willie for the first time one of the all-time most exciting moments of her life.

Willie introduced Roger Miller and Bob Dylan in the audience and went on to say, "And Marshall Chapman, a young singer from Nashville." Marshall remembers that she "nearly fell out of [her] seat!" Later, Willie and a group of other people, including Marshall, went to the aviary on the old John Barrymore Estate, where Roger Miller was staying at the time. During the evening, a guitar was passed from one to the other for impromptu performances. Marshall sang "A Woman's Heart (Is a Handy Place to Be)." Roger quipped to Willie (quoting a line from the song, "Runnin' from a friend to find a stranger"), "That ain't bad!" Marshall felt at that moment that she could really be a songwriter.

Marshall's voice is sultry, honest, earthy and engaging. When you hear her sing, you know she has lived these emotions and they're never artificial. Even with the blues, Marshall Chapman pulls you into her world, spins you around and sends you out better than you were before—because she's just that kind of person.

That winter, she went to Ketchum, Idaho, to ski during the day and play music at night. The next year, 1975, she spent in Boston.

Marshall's first album, *Me, I'm Fellin' Free*, was released on Epic Records in 1977. Her second, *Jaded Virgin*, came out in 1978 and was voted "Record of the Year" by *Stereo Review*.

Since then, Marshall's songs have been recorded by people such as Conway Twitty, Jimmy Buffet, Joe Cocker, Emmylou Harris, Tanya Tucker, John Hiatt, Jessi Colter, Olivia Newton-John, Dion, Ronnie Milsap and Irma Thomas with Sawyer Brown reaching number one with "Betty's Bein' Bad."

Marshall has recorded eleven more albums since *Jaded Virgin. Marshall* (Epic, 1979), *Take It on Home* (Rounder, 1982), *Dirty Linen* (TallGirl/Line Import, 1987) and *Inside Job* (Tallgirl, 1991) were followed by *It's About Time…* (Island/Margaritaville, 1995) recorded live at Tennesseee State Prison for Women. *It's About Time…* drew rave reviews from folks at *USA Today*, *Time* and the *Village Voice*.

Marshall's next albums were *Love Slave* (Island, 1996); *Goodbye, Little Rock-and-Roller* (Tallgirl, 2003), an accompaniment for her book by the same name; *Live! The Bitter End* (Tallgirl, 2004); *Mellowicious!* (Thirty Tigers/Tallgirl, 2006); and *Big Lonesome* (Tallgirl, 2010). *Big Lonesome* was written after Marshall suffered the loss of a close friend and fellow songwriter with whom she had performed many times. It is a superb album, one of her best.

Marshall Chapman and Tim Krekel were writing, singing and music-making buddies for many years, so when Tim was diagnosed with cancer and consequently died only three months later, it was a huge hurt for Marshall Chapman. Although she had begun to devote her time to writing books and had vowed never to make another CD, the songs began to blossom without warning, and *Big Lonesome* was born.

In May 2013, Marshall's *Blaze of Glory* (Tallgirl) featured "Love in the Wind" (written with Todd Snider), "I Don't Want Nobody," "Nearness of You," "Beyond Words," "Let's Make Waves," "Dreams & Memories," "Blues Stay Away from Me," "Waiting for the Music," "Call the Lamas," "Not Afraid to Die" and "Blaze of Glory." The album has taken off and has a life of its own.

"Call the Lamas" was also featured on *Goodbye, Little Rock-and-Roller*; it is a charming song about seeing a Buddha baby in a grocery cart as he smiles beatifically at three little girls who are swirling around their mother's knees. The song is in total contrast to many of Marshall's deep-felt cries of pathos or passionate love songs. It was written as her brother was dying, and she came to recognize that the three little girls in the grocery who were mesmerized by the baby represented Marshall and her sisters kissing her brother good-bye.

*Blaze of Glory* is just that. It is on fire on the charts and has three songs being played by Starbucks. Marshall Chapman is an "overnight [after quite a number of years at paying her dues] success."

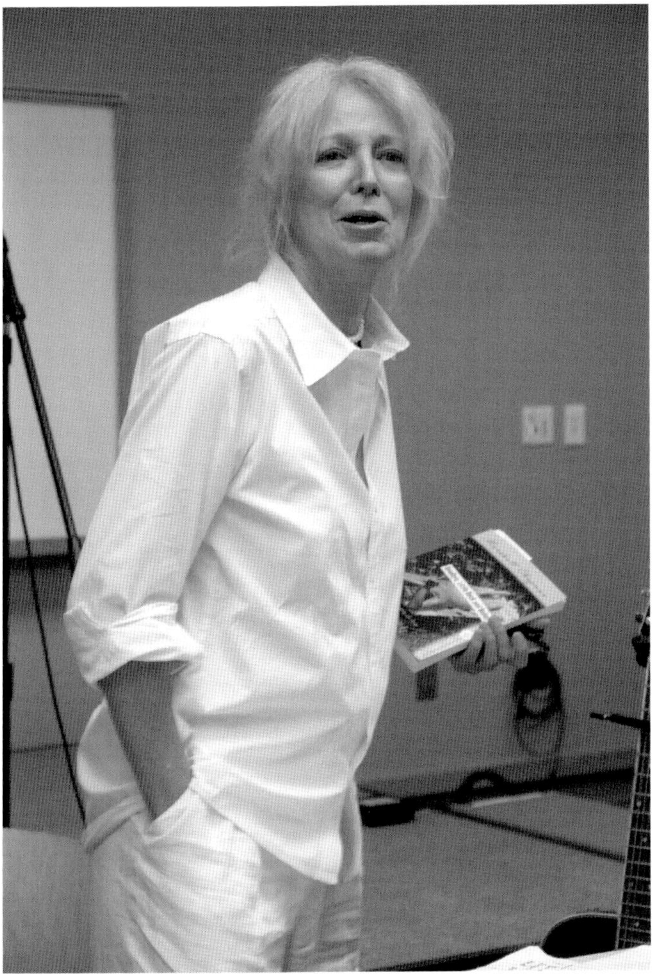

Marshall Chapman answers questions from other writers. *Bill Larson.*

Marshall's second book, *They Came to Nashville*, (Vanderbilt University Press–Country Music Foundation Press), was a 2010 Fall Okra Pick and a winner of the 2011 Book Award of the Southern Independent Booksellers Association. It was also a Pulpwood Queens Book Club selection for January 2011.

*Happiness is wanting what you have, not having what you want.*
*Can I have a witness?*
*Do I hear an Amen?*
*Marshall Chapman,* Goodbye, Little Rock-and-Roller

## SECOND BOOK

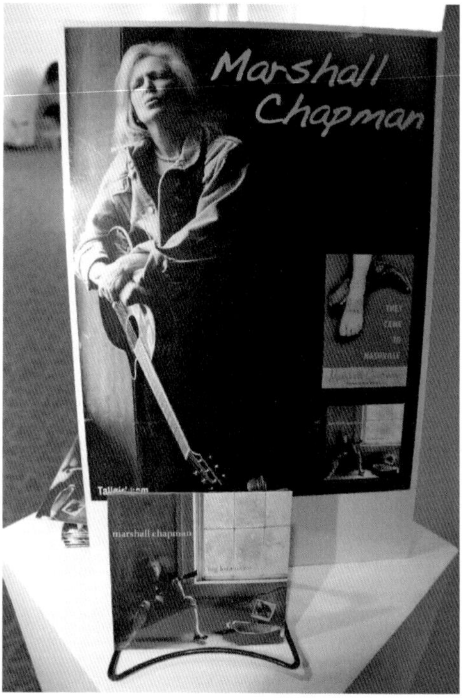


One of Marshall Chapman's CDs. *Bill Larson.*

*They Came to Nashville* features interviews with people such as Kris Kristofferson, Emmylou Harris and Miranda Lambert, and the book searches their reasons for not only coming to Nashville but also sticking with their career dreams through thick and thin. After forty years as a Nashville resident, Marshall knows everyone there is to know, and her immediate intimacy with no holds barred gives her access to secrets that people are willing to share with her alone. The last chapter of the book reveals her tour bus ride with Willie Nelson and her various attempts at trying to get enough time to interview him on his 2008 ride through America; she ends up on stage with Willie in Beaumont, Texas, singing "Good Hearted Woman." The book is a must read for anyone who wants a glimpse into what makes Nashville "Music City" and the characters who give it that moniker.

Marshall's writing career extends to being a contributing editor for *Nashville Arts* magazine and *Garden & Gun*. She has also written for *W*, *Southern Living*, the *Oxford American*, *Performing Songwriter* and the *Bob Edwards Show* on Sirius/XM. Her voice is as clear on paper as it is in song. Her honesty and emotion always come through.

## BUSY LIFE

Stories about Marshall are rampant. She admits to planting her front yard with garden vegetables (a fact her West End neighbors have varying opinions about), going out during the terrible flood of Nashville in 2010 in nothing but a pink shower cap to remove the leaves from her gutter so that her basement wouldn't flood (it didn't) and numerous other escapades throughout her life. Marshall embraces life, lives hers with gusto and looks back with unjaded eyes.

In 1998, Marshall and Matraca Berg wrote fourteen songs for the country musical *Good Ol' Girls*, based on stories by Lee Smith and Jill McCorkle. The musical is being performed throughout the South to rave reviews.

In January 2010, she landed her first movie role, playing Gwyneth Paltrow's road manager in *Country Strong*. She also appeared on the television show *Nashville* on April 24, 2013; it was shot on the *General Jackson* on the Cumberland River in the heart of Nashville.

No discussion of the life of Marshall Chapman would be complete without the mention of her husband, Chris Fletcher. Chris is definitely the "wind beneath her wings." When they are in public, he is smoothing the path for her at every turn. Whether it's collecting money for her books and CDs or making sure the mike is right, Chris is there for Marshall's every need. After all, he's the one who told her in no uncertain terms to get on that bus with Willie Nelson after she had originally turned down the chance. As Marshall later said, "You don't have to be smokin' to get high on that bus!"

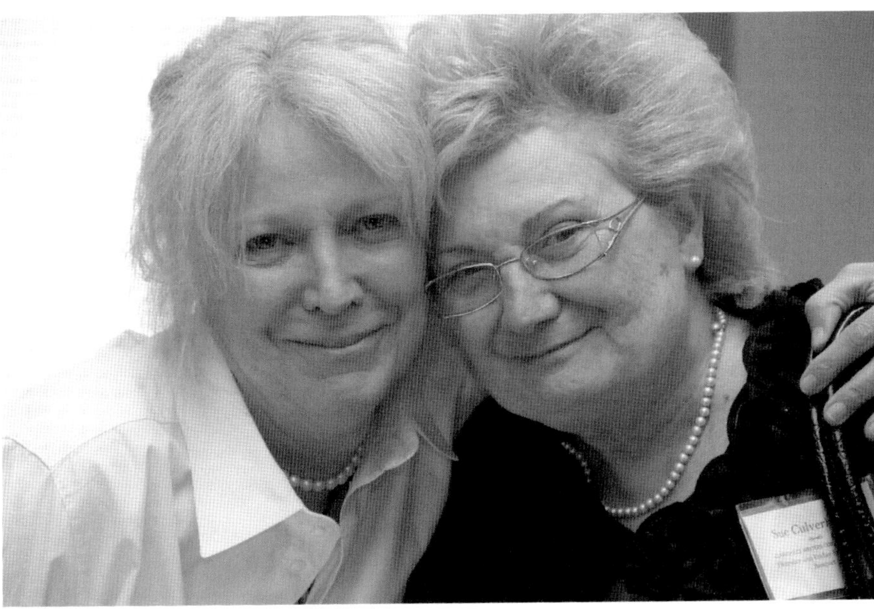

Marshall Chapman with me. *Bill Larson.*

Her chapter in *They Came to Nashville* called "Riding with Willie" is not one you'll want to miss.

> *When you're going in style, it doesn't much matter where you're going.*
> *Marshall Chapman,* Goodbye, Little Rock-and-Roller

Marshall Chapman is pure Nashville these days, birthplace in South Carolina or not. Her frequent trips to Mexico influence her songs and her ever-touring schedule with her band, the Love Slaves, keeps her busy, but it's Nashville that calls her back. Whether she's hanging out with her legendary record producer–songwriter friend Cowboy Jack Clement or laying down some track on Music Row, Marshall Chapman has come home.

# BIBLIOGRAPHY

This bibliography is a list of some of the books I have read and some I plan to read in the future. It is meant to be, not an all-inclusive resource collection, but a guide for others who wish to read about these remarkable Tennesseans. Their complete works are listed, for the most part, in each chapter.

## Chapter One

Allen, Patrick, ed. *Literary Nashville*. Athens, GA: Hill Street Press, 1999.

Ballard, Ernie. "*The Southern Review* Celebrates 75 Years of Literary Excellence." *LSU Gold*. www.lsu.edu/departments/gold/2010/12/review.shtml.

Blotner, Joseph. *Robert Penn Warren: A Biography*. New York: Random House, 1997.

Clark, William Bedford, ed. *Selected Letters of Robert Penn Warren: The Apprentice Years, 1924–1934*. Vol. 1. Baton Rouge: Louisiana State University Press, 2000.

———. *Selected Letters of Robert Penn Warren: The* Southern Review *Years, 1935–1942*. Vol. 2. Baton Rouge: Louisiana State University Press, 2001.

Corlew, Robert E., and William B. Wheeler. *Tennessee: The Volunteer State*. Sun Valley, CA: American Historical Press, 2008.

*The Fugitives*. Documentary by Nashville Public Television. This NPT original production was made possible by a grant from the Metropolitan Nashville Arts Commission. 2008. video.wnpt.org/video/2242870204/

Gregory, Rick. "Black Patch War." *Tennessee Encyclopedia of History and Culture*. www.tennesseeencyclopedia.net.

Grimshaw, James A., Jr. "Introduction." *Robert Penn Warren: A Documentary Volume*. Edited by James A. Grimshaw Jr. Dictionary of Literary Biography, 320. Farmington Hills, MI: Gale, 2006. Reprinted online. www.robertpennwarren.com/RPW-A%20Documentary%20Volume.

"Honors." Robert Penn Warren, 1905–1989. www.robertpennwarren.com/honors.htm.

Landess, Thomas. "Meeting the Men Behind *I'll Take My Stand*." *American Conservative*, May 17, 2011, www.theamericanconservative.com/articles/fugitive-agrarians/.

McGill, Ralph. "Formaldehyde and Poetry." *Literary Nashville*: 83–94. Reprinted from *the South* and the *Southerner*. University of Georgia Press, 1992.

Murphy, Paul V. "Introduction." *The Rebuke of History: The Southern Agrarians and American Conservative Thought*. Chapel Hill: University of North Carolina Press, 2001. www.ibiblio.org/uncpress/chapters/murphy_rebuke.html

Murray, Miles. "Tobacco." *Tennessee Encyclopedia of History and Culture*. www.tennesseeencyclopedia.net.

*National Observer*. March 12, 1977. Quote from beginning, "I've been a lot of places..."

Netz, Genevieve L. "Guthrie, KY: A Railroad Town." Prairie Bluestem, September 21, 2007. www.prairiebluestem.blogspot.com/2007/09/guthrie-ky-railroad-town.html; list of railroads in Guthrie, Kentucky.

Robert Penn Warren Collection. Donated by Patricia and Howard Winn. Special Collections. Austin Peay State University Felix G. Woodward Library. Clarksville, TN.

Stacey, Sandra J. Martin. *Clarksville-Montgomery County Schools: Pictorial & Historical Collection*. Vol. 2. 1999.

Sullivan, Walter. "Behind the Iron Mask: Joseph Blotner's Warren." *Virginia Quarterly Review* (Autumn 1997): 729–34.

Warren, Robert Penn. *All the King's Men*. New York: Harcourt Brace and Company, Inc., 1946.

———. *The Circus in the Attic and Other Stories*. San Diego, CA: Harcourt Brace Jovanovich, 1947.

———. *Night Rider*. Boston, MA: Houghton Mifflin, 1939.

———. *A Portrait of a Father*. Lexington: University Press of Kentucky, 1988. (Originally published in *Southern Review* [Spring 1987]: 33).

———. *Segregation: The Inner Conflict in the South* New York: Random House, 1956.

———. *Who Speaks for the Negro*. New York: Random House, 1965.

———. *Wilderness*. New York: Random House, 1961.
Watkins, Floyd C., John T. Hiers, and Mary Louise Weaks. *Talking with Robert Penn Warren*. Athens: University of Georgia Press, 1990.
Winn, Thomas H. "The *Night Rider* Revisited: A Historical Perspective." *Southern Quarterly* 31, no. 4 (Summer 1993).
———. "*Night Riders* and Tobacco Wars: A Review Essay." *Southern Quarterly* 33, no. 1 (Fall 1994).
Young, Thomas Daniel. *Tennessee Writers*. Knoxville: University of Tennessee Press, 1981.

## CHAPTER TWO

Goodwin, Stephen. "An Interview with Peter Taylor." *Shenandoah* 24 (Winter, 1973): 3–20. Copyright by Washington and Lee University, reprinted from *Shenandoah: The Washington and Lee University Review* with the permission of the editor in McAlexander's *Conversations with Peter Taylor*.
Howard, Elizabeth. "A Visit with Peter Taylor." *Albemarle Monthly* 1, no. 2 (June 1, 1978).
McAlexander, Hubert H., ed. *Conversations with Peter Taylor*. Oxford: University Press of Mississippi, 1987.
———. *Peter Taylor: A Writer's Life*. Baton Rouge: Louisiana State University Press, 2001.
McKenzie, Bryan. "Esteemed Poet Eleanor Taylor Dies," *(Charlottesville, VA) Daily Progress*, January 3, 2012. http://www2.dailyprogress.com/news/2012/jan/03/esteemed-poet-eleanor-taylor-dies-ar-1585126
Powell, Dannye Romine. "Poet Eleanor Ross Taylor Dies. *Charlotte (NC) Observer*, January 3, 2012. www.charlotteobserver.com/2012/01/03/2894402/poet-eleanor-ross-taylor-dies.html.
Taylor, Eleanor Ross. *Captive Voices: New and Selected Poems.* Baton Rouge: Louisiana State University Press, 2009.
———. *Wilderness of Ladies*. New York: McDowell, Obolensky, 1960.
Taylor, Peter. *The Collected Stories of Peter Taylor*. New York: Farrar, Straus and Giroux, 1969.
———. *In the Miro District and Other Stories*. New York: Alfred A. Knopf, 1977.
———. *In the Tennessee Country*. New York: Alfred A. Knopf, 1994.
———. *A Summons to Memphis*. New York: Alfred A. Knopf, 1986.
———. *A Woman of Means.* New York: Harcourt, Brace, 1950.

## Chapter Three

GradeSaver. "Biography of Cormac McCarthy (1933–)." www.gradesaver.com/author/cormac-mccarthy/.

McCarthy, Cormac. *All the Pretty Horses*. New York: Alfred A. Knopf, 1992.

———. *Blood Meridian; or, The Evening Redness in the West*. New York: Random House, 1985.

———. *Child of God*. New York: Random House, 1973.

———. *Cities of the Plain*. New York: Alfred A. Knopf, 1998.

———. *The Crossing*. New York: Alfred A. Knopf, 1994.

———. *No Country for Old Men*. New York: Alfred A. Knopf, 2005.

———. *Outer Dark*. New York: Random House, 1968.

———. *Suttree*. New York: Random House, 1979.

———. *The Orchard Keeper*. New York, Random House, 1965.

———. *The Road*. New York: Alfred A. Knopf, 2006.

———. *The Stonemason*. New York: Ecco Press, 1994.

The Official Site of the Cormac McCarthy Society. www.cormacmccarthy.com.

Woodward, Richard B. "Cormac McCarthy's Venomous Fiction." *New York Times*, April 19, 1992. www.nytimes.com/1992/04/19/books/mccarthy-venomous.html?pagewanted=all&emc=eta1.

## Chapter Four

Brewer, Sonny, ed. *Don't Quit Your Day Job: Acclaimed Authors and the Day Jobs They Quit*. Isle of Man, UK: M.P. Publishing Limited, Douglas, 2011.

Chapman, Marshall. "William, Another View." Best of the South, 2012. *Oxford American* 77: 113–15.

Culverhouse, Sue Freeman. "An Accidental Meeting with William Gay." *Clarksville Online*, August 4, 2010. http://www.clarksvilleonline.com/2010/08/04/an-accidental-meeting-with-william-gay/.

———. "A Glimpse of William Gay." *Clarksville Online*, July 18, 2011. www.clarksvilleonline.com/2011/07/18/a-glimpse-of-william-gay/.

———. "Memories of William Gay with Sonny Brewer and William's Son, Chris." *Clarksville Online*, July 3, 2012. http://www.clarksvilleonline.com/2012/07/03/memories-of-william-gay-with-sonny-brewer-and-williams-son-chris/.

———. "On the Passing of William Gay." *Clarksville Online*, February 25, 2012. http://www.clarksvilleonline.com/2012/02/25/on-the-passing-of-william-gay/.

———. "A Tribute to the Life of William Gay." *Clarksville Online*, June 27, 2012. http://www.clarksvilleonline.com/2012/06/27/a-tribute-to-the-life-of-william-gay/.

Franklin, Tom. "William Gay (1941–2012): A Tribute." *Oxford American*, March 8, 2012. http://www.oxfordamerican.org/articles/2012/mar/08/william-gay-19422012-tribute/.

Gay, William. *I Hate to See That Evening Sun Go Down*. New York: Free Press, 2002.

———. *The Long Home*. Denver, CO: MacMurray and Beck, 1999.

———. *Provinces of Night*. New York: Doubleday, 2000.

———. *Time Done Been Won't Be No More*. Edited by J.M. White. Brush Creek, TN: Wild Dog Press, 2010.

———. *Twilight*. San Francisco, CA: MacAdam/Cage, 2006.

———. *Wittgenstein's Lolita/The Iceman*. Brush Creek, TN: Wild Dog Press, 2006.

Giraldi, William. "The World Almost Rotten: The Fiction of William Gay." *Southern Review* (2008). Reprinted in *Rumpus*, April 18, 2012. www.therumpus.net/2012/04/a-world-almost-rotten-the-fiction-of-william-gay/

Rawson, Keith. "An Interview with William Gay." *Lit Reactor*, December 20, 2011. www.litreactor.com/interviews/an-interview-with-william-gay.

Ridley, Jim. "William Gay, Acclaimed Tennessee Author, Dead at 68," *Nashville Scene*, February 24, 2012. www.nashvillescene.com/countrylife/archives/2012/02/24/william-gay-acclaimed-tennessee-author-dead-at-68.

Shapiro, T. Rees. "Author William Gay Dies at 70." *Washington Post*, March 1, 2012. www.washingtonpost.com/entertainment/books/author-william-gay-dies-at-93/2012/03/01/gIQAmL.

Stamper, Jeff. "Positively William Gay." *Nashville Arts*, December 4, 2009. www.nashvillearts.com/2009/12/04/positively-william-gay/.

Weber, Bruce. "William Gay Dies at 70; Writer Tied to Tennessee." *New York Times*, February 29, 2012. www.nytimes.com/2012/03/01/arts/william-gay-novelist-rooted-in-tennessee-dies-at-70.html?pagewanted=all.

Zacharias, Karen Spears. "The Brilliant Gay." Patheos, February 25, 2012. www.patheos.com/blogs/karenspearszacharias/2012/02/25/the-brilliant-gay/.

Note: A complete bibliography of all William Gay's publications can be found in *Time Done Been Won't Be No More* as compiled by his great friend J.M. (Michael) White.

## CHAPTER FIVE

Books and Writers. "Alex Palmer Haley (1921–1992)." www.kirjasto.sci.fi/ahaley.

Greene, Terry. "The Anguish of Alex Haley's Widow: With Her Husband's Literary Legacy Dispersed, She's Locked in a Bitter Probate Battle." *Phoenix New Times*, November 11 1992. www.phoenixnewtimes.com.

Haley, Alex. *A Different Kind of Christmas*. New York: Doubleday, 1988.

———. *Queen: The Story of an American Family*. New York: William Morrow and Company, 1993.

———. *Roots*. New York: Doubleday, 1976.

Letter from Alex Haley to Stephen Ambrose and Doris Kearns Goodwin. hnn.us/articles/539.html.

Pace, Eric. Obituary of Alex Haley. February 11, 1992. www.nytimes.com/learning/general/onthisday/bday/0811.html.

## CHAPTER SIX

Culverhouse, Sue Freeman. "An Afternoon with Lee and Bud Willis and Friends." *Clarksville Online*, June 5, 2011. www.clarksvilleonline.com/2011/06/05/serendipity%E2%80%94an-afternoon-with-lee-and-bud-willis-and-friends/.

———. "Blue Stocking—A Family Story with a Tennessee Heart." *Clarksville Online*, July 2, 2011. www.clarksvilleonline.com/2011/07/02/bluestocking-%E2%80%94-a-family-story-with-a-tennessee-heart/.

———. "Former Clarksvillian Bud Willis Wins Major Literary Award." *Clarksville Online*, October, 1, 2012. www.clarksvilleonline.com/2012/10/01/former-clarksvillian-bud-willis-wins-major-literary-award/.

———. "Marble Mountain: A Vietnam Memoir is Unforgettable." *Clarksville Online*, May 31, 2011. www.clarksvilleonline.com/2011/05/31/marble-mountain-a-vietnam-memoir-is-unforgettable/.

Willis, Bud. *Bluestocking*. Bloomington, IN: AuthorHouse, 2009.

———. *Marble Mountain: A Vietnam Memoir*. Bloomington, IN: AuthorHouse, 2011.

## Chapter Seven

Alice Randall's website. http://www.alicerandall.com/.

Culverhouse, Sue Freeman. "Eighth Clarksville Writers' Conference 2012: Renaissance Woman Alice Randall Describes *Ada's Rules*." *Clarksville Online*, July 2, 2012. www.clarksvilleonline.com/2012/07/02/eighth-clarksville-writers-conference-2012-renaissance-woman-alice-randall-describes-adas-rules/.

———. "Renaissance Woman Alice Randall." *Clarksville Online*, August 19, 2010. www.clarksvilleonline.com/2010/08/19/renaissance-woman-alice-randall/.

Randall, Alice. *Ada's Rules*. New York: Bloomsbury, 2012.

———. *Pushkin and the Queen of Spades*. New York: Houghton Mifflin, 2004.

———. *Rebel Yell*. New York: Bloomsbury, 2009.

———. *The Wind Done Gone*. New York: Houghton Mifflin Harcourt, 2001.

## Chapter Eight

Amy Greene's website. http://amygreeneauthor.com/.

Culverhouse, Sue Freeman. "Amy Greene a New Star on the Writing Horizon." *Clarksville Online*, July 19, 2011. www.clarksvilleonline.com/2011/07/19/amy-greene-a-new-star-on-the-writing-horizon/.

Greene, Amy. *Bloodroot*. New York: Alfred A. Knopf, 2010.

Haupt, Jennifer. "Interview with Author Amy Greene." One True Thing. *Psychology Today*, February 26, 2011. http://www.psychologytoday.com/blog/one-true-thing/201102/interview-author-amy-greene.

## Chapter Nine

A. Scott Pearson's website. www.ascottpearson.com/.

Culverhouse, Sue Freeman. "A. Scott Pearson: Surgeon, Cancer Researcher, Patient Advocate and Novelist." *Clarksville Online*, August 13, 2010. www.clarksvilleonline.com/2010/08/13/a-scott-pearson-surgeon-cancer-researcher-patient-advocate-and-novelist/.

———. "Eighth Clarksville Writers' Conference 2012: A. Scott Pearson Wins Benjamin Franklin Award for Mysteries." *Clarksville Online*, June 16, 2016. www.clarksvilleonline.com/2012/06/16/eighth-clarksville-writers-conference-2012-a-scott-pearson-wins-benjamin-franklin-award-for-mysteries/.

Pearson A.S., M.P. McTigue, and J.L. Tarpley. "Narrative Medicine in surgical Education." *Journal of Surgical Medicine* 65, no. 2 (March–April 2008): 99–100.

Pearson, A. Scott. *Public Anatomy*. Ipswich, MA: Oceanview Publishing, 2011.

———. *Rupture*. Ipswich, MA: Oceanview Publishing, 2010.

Peterson, Andrew. "*Public Anatomy* by A. Scott Pearson." Big Thrill, January 28, 2009. www.thebigthrill.org/2011/02/public-anatomy-by-a-scott-pearson/.

Stewart, Michael F. "*Public Anatomy* by A. Scott Pearson." Big Thrill. http://www.thebigthrill.org/2011/02/public-anatomy-by-a-scott-pearson/.

Zeringue, Marshal. "A. Scott Pearson's 'Rupture.'" My Book, the Movie, February 25, 2009. mybookthemovie.blogspot.com/2009/02/scott-pearsons-rupture.html.

## Chapter Ten

Chapman, Marshall. *Goodbye, Little Rock-and-Roller.* New York: St. Martin's Press, 2003.

———. *They Came to Nashville.* Nashville, TN: Vanderbilt University Press and Country Music Foundation Press, 2010.

Culverhouse, Sue Freeman. "Marshall Chapman's CD *Big Lonesome* Takes You to the Blues and Back." *Clarksville Online*, July 10, 2012. www.clarksvilleonline.com/2012/07/10/marshall-chapmans-cd-big-lonesome-takes-you-to-the-blues-and-back/.

———. "Marshall Chapman's New *Blaze of Glory* CD." *Clarksvile Online*, May 17, 2013. www.clarksvilleonline.com/2013/05/17/marshall-chapmans-new-blaze-of-glory-cd/.

Marshall Chapman's website. www.TallGirl.com/.

# ABOUT THE AUTHOR

Sue Freeman Culverhouse is a freelance writer who lives in Springfield, Tennessee, with her lawyer-sculptor husband, Bill Culverhouse. She is the author of *Seven Keys to a Successful Life*, a self-help book, and *To Cure Sometimes, To Comfort Always*, the history of Blue Ridge Hospital, now a part of the Medical Center library at the University of Virginia.

Sue is also author of articles in the following magazines: *American Horticulturist*, *Flower and Garden*, *Historic Preservation*, *Americana* magazine,

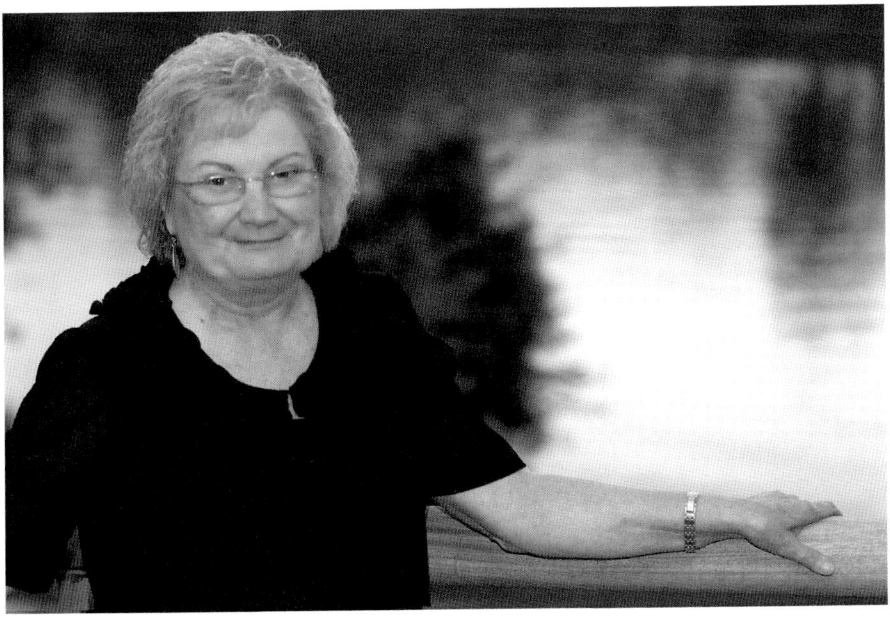

*Envirosouth*, *National Mall Monitor*, *Quilt World*, the *Tennessee Churchman*, *Grit*, *Albemarle Monthly*, *Greenleaves*, *Albemarle* magazine, *Unity* magazine, *Teach* (Tennessee Education Association magazine) and *Humpty Dumpty* magazine.

Her work in newspapers gleaned two Virginia Press Awards. Sue's columns have appeared in the following newspapers: the *News-Virginian*, Waynesboro, Virginia; the *Daily Progress*, Charlottesville, Virginia; and the *Robertson County Times*, Springfield, Tennessee. Sue is a staffwriter for clarksvilleonline.com in Clarksville, Tennessee.

Having taught in public school for sixteen years, Sue created the first literary magazine for children at Watauga Elementary School, where she teaches music and writing.

*Visit us at*
www.historypress.net

*This title is also available as an e-book*